MORE THAN

a story

ONE THING

of survival

CAN BE TRUE

CAROLINE BRUNNE

First published by CGB Management Pty Ltd in 2022

carolinebrunne.com

Some names and distinguishing details have been changed.

ISBN: 978-0-6454436-0-8

A catalogue entry for this book is available from the National Library of Australia.

Cover design by Kerry Cooke
Cover image by Adobe Stock/Slonme
Author photograph by Melissa Martin
Internal design by Kerry Cooke
Typeset in 10pt/18pt Caecilla LT Std 45 Light by Kerry Cooke
Printed and bound in Australia by IngramSpark

CGB Management acknowledge that Aboriginal and Torres Strait Islander peoples are the Traditional Custodians and the first storytellers of the lands on which we live and work. We honour Aboriginal and Torres Strait Island peoples' continuous connection to Country, waters, skies and communities. We celebrate Aboriginal and Torres Strait Islander stories, traditions and living cultures; and we pay our respects to Elders past and present.

DEDICATION

To ten-year-old Caroline, I dedicate this book to you. I acknowledge everything you have lost, and thank you for everything you have given me through your strength and courage.

The secrets you have carried will no longer weigh you down; today you are free.

I love you.

PREFACE

It's a tightrope. While I look at the women in the world today speaking up when they say, 'Enough is enough,' and commend them, I know how difficult it is to find the courage to press on. But at the same time, it can be overwhelming as I watch these women disclose their hidden secrets. The telling of their truth is an exposé of the abuse of power and a level of corruption that is rife in our governments, schools, churches, sporting clubs, families and yes, even in our very own homes. Similar to the individuals who occupy these organisations and collective bodies, these systems and institutions can be more than one thing; brilliant in their purpose and success and catastrophically flawed in their lack of accountability and justice for survivors.

In my sacrifice and choice to live in this space, when the mainland I lived on became the arena. My parents were in the box seats, dictating, many times without words, the human sacrifice I needed to make to uphold the structure of our space. The sacrifice I needed to make to convince the world that everything was ok, that we were *normal*. The message was that the institution and structure of family and its importance far outweigh the value of one's life, one sole life, my life. Rules of moving on past the abuse, staying quiet and still succeeding in society were unspoken, though behaviours were modelled and expectations were clear. I showed up, day after day, led by my parents and played the role I was expected to play. I was the good girl, the perfect daughter, the clever girl who would go on to be a successful woman. The actor continued to act, regardless of whether I knew that my role was fictional or if I believed this to be my one true life. I would not speak a word, I would not make a sound, I would continue to follow the rules.

In my choice to no longer be silent about the abuse, I understand that I have shifted the focus away from the shining neon signs of my strategic achievements. I have instead shone a light on the dark underbelly that I could no longer escape. I have acknowledged and come to terms with the fact that I cannot acknowledge and be who I am today without my lived experience; there is no other option but to live this life that I have been given. To acknowledge the trauma, survive it and go on to thrive despite the pain.

I have spent my entire life putting myself and the versions of me into boxes, boxes behind walls, boxes inside of boxes. All to protect myself from further hurt and disappointment. Releasing Caroline, every version of her, has given me the freedom to be whole again. I am no longer boxes inside of boxes. I am one fully formed being, whole, fully formed in my truth.

One

CAROLINE, THE CHILD

'Tell me about your childhood,' the interviewer asked. We were recording a podcast and I had heard this question many times over the months where I had been working to create a marketing buzz around my new business, using the power of public relations and word of mouth to share my story. I've been a business owner and entrepreneur for many years. I am well-versed in the answer that always comes, after having spoken and written about my childhood so many times. I have spent countless hours in interviews explaining how I became the woman I am today and how my childhood has played a part in my business skills, most importantly in my organisation skills.

'I come from a really big family and that was the core of my event management skills, which is how I learned to embrace the power of navigating larger groups of people. Growing up and always having family around created the mini event manager in me,' I would routinely repeat, time and time again.

Those who have read those interviews or have listened to my words won't be shocked by the fact that yes, I do indeed have 28 first cousins. My parents are both one of eight children, so it isn't hard to imagine that eventually, when all of those aunts and uncles got married and had children of their own that there would be 31 of us nestled on our family tree, on our collective generational branches.

Being from such a big family meant many large family gatherings. These gatherings became the blueprint for my skills in event and time management, and those skills would go on to be vital to the success of my business. They were planted somewhere deep inside of me and I turned them into a profitable career and business path. I've spent years mastering my craft and becoming known as the most organised person in the room, mastering my ability for control. Though the framework of a large extended family has been a major part of my life, the need for control has played an even greater part in my development.

In many ways I am glad that in each interview the interviewer has not questioned me on what I was *really* like as a child, or more specifically, what I wanted to do when I grew up. To be honest, I don't think I could have answered such questions wholeheartedly. I have had a fragmented memory of my childhood for my entire adult life. There are pieces of my childhood that I simply need to forget so I can exist in my body. There are pieces of my history that I simply wish were not my reality. This is common for people who have experienced childhood sexual abuse. I often refer to my lack of clear memories as my trauma brain. Referring to my brain in this way reminds me that my lack of memory is due to the long-lasting impacts of my childhood trauma, not simply a random case of forgetfulness. I am someone who prides myself on my excellent attention to detail and my capability to memorise specific tasks and occurrences, so the fact that I have so many black spots and holes in my personal memories is utterly devastating.

Similar to most people who lived their childhood in the '80s and '90s in middle-class Australia, I have many photos and videos of the different versions of me as I grew, from the scrawny immigrant girl to the curvy, confident woman I am today. I was fortunate that my parents took great pride in technology, so from a very young age there are photos of me growing up in

Mauritius, our tiny island home off the coast of South Africa where I was born. There are beautiful memories captured of me with my older brother posing at birthday parties, dancing with friends, and spending time at the beach surrounded by loving family members. We lived in a beautiful part of the world; the kind of paradise that people have photos of in their homes, depicting where they wish they could be. We were also a fortunate family from what I've been told. My parents worked hard to provide for us and took the opportunities that opened up to them. From what my brother has shared with me, life was good. The photos are evidence of a good childhood.

One old photo I love looking at is my passport photo from when we were migrating to Australia in the late 1980s. It is the standard, don't-smile-for-the-camera type of photo required for a passport. When I look at that photo, I think I look pretty darn cute, even though I'm not smiling. I look at that little girl version of myself, the version who could barely speak any English, the version who was about to start a whole new life in another country and I wish I knew what had been going on in my little brain. Was I excited? Was I scared? Did I understand how different it would be growing up in Australia? So much for a little person to take on, an overwhelming set of changes to come for me. There was so much hope and opportunity, but also so much uncertainty ahead. I see it in my eyes when I look at this photo; I am both cute and I am unsure, I am more than one thing.

Then there are the photos of us in Australia, looking awkward as immigrant children sometimes do in a new place. I am luckily still surrounded by family as many of our family members had migrated to Victoria prior to us moving, which meant we had the opportunity to live with them before settling into our very own home as we began to live the Australian dream.

When I really stretch myself, when I pull at the memories that are hidden in the depths of my trauma brain, I can remember the feelings of struggle, mainly with language and wanting so desperately to belong. I also remember the feelings of admiration I had for my older cousins who had in part taken me under their wing. The cousins who already called Australia home, who had friends and seemed so cool and together. They already seemed like they had a sense of belonging and somewhere in my subconscious I knew I had to mimic their behaviour so I could fit in as soon as possible. Fitting in was important, being the good girl and belonging was a vital part of my need to survive.

These photos and videos help jog my memory, they provide me with concrete evidence of the life I have had. They help me remember that my childhood was in many ways rather normal, well, my version of normal, being an immigrant in Australia in the 1980s. Being an immigrant didn't spare me from iconic hair and crazy fashion choices and all of the other wonderful things the '80s and '90s are known for. The timestamps in these visuals, the clothing, the hair and the overall aesthetic of this point in time are featured in these photos. These photos are living proof of what was and who I was. Or more to the point, who I could have continued to be if trauma wasn't right around the corner, waiting to change my life forever.

There is a beauty in the innocence I see in those photos of my childhood, a freedom that at times only youth can give us. Before the world gets in the way, before we are exposed to the things that cause the scars that we carry forever, bending and shaping the beings we will become. They are the proof of my childhood; the proof of what life was like before I lived in two worlds.

I was born on Christmas Eve. Due to the French influence in my Mauritian heritage, as a child we celebrated Christmas on the 24th of December. My parents always made a point to ensure my birthday was never overshadowed by our Christmas celebrations, and this meant my birthdays were a big deal.

I remember one epic year, when most of my family had migrated from Mauritius to Australia, we celebrated my birthday at our family home. Starting with a birthday party where friends from school were invited and flowing on into the night when the party turned from birthday celebrations to a Christmas extravaganza. Later that evening, in our backyard, surrounded by my parents, siblings, uncles, aunts and cousins, Santa arrived to the squeals and excitement of all of the children who hurried to find a place to sit at his feet in hopes of receiving a present. That night, each and every child received a present from Santa and because I was celebrating two-fold I remember proudly carrying massive bags full of gifts back to my bedroom after the thrilling 24-hour celebration of my birthday and Christmas. Later that night, after lots of eating, singing and dancing I fell asleep wherever my head landed as my parents and the other adults partied into the night. It was my '80s life at its best and this memory still fills me with so much delight.

This innocence of being so thrilled at receiving so many gifts and cards filled with words of love and good wishes was coupled with the freedom to sleep so safe and sound at the end of an exciting day. I don't think I will ever forget those moments; they are the peak of my childhood joy. They are the memories where I can close my eyes and really feel the moment, transporting myself to the joy of my childhood. To the feeling of being so small, but feeling so full of love, knowing I was a part of something so much bigger than me. These are the moments I so wish I could relive, time and time again.

Around this time of my life my little sister was born. I know some children pester their parents for a little brother or sister but I don't recall that being my experience. With an older brother and a sea of cousins to spend time with I don't remember ever craving the connection of a little sister. However, when my sister arrived, changing our family forever and making me a middle child, I knew that I loved her. I loved my sister in a way I had never loved anyone before. It was a giddy love, full of excitement for the experiences to come as we united in our sisterhood. Maybe it was a female thing, the bond I found in a sibling the same sex as me, maybe it was something else, something maternal almost. I do remember how naturally it came to me to simply look after my sister, to be her protector and keeper from the very beginning. There is nothing quite like the bond of sisters and this new addition to our family would change me forever, and for the better. I believe I am a better woman because I am a big sister.

Soon after this point in time there was a shift in our family, in what seemed like a hasty decision we were suddenly moving from Victoria to Queensland. I don't recall a major discussion about the move, or really knowing why we were moving. We didn't have any family in Queensland. My aunts, uncles and cousins were all living in Victoria and it felt like we would be starting again in another foreign place where we didn't quite belong. I was assured by my parents that it would be wonderful and that the climate in Queensland was similar to Mauritius. This was an appealing part of the relocation, to escape the bitter cold of the long Victorian winters and the unpredictable nature of the weather. I was never told why we were moving away; this was not a decision for children to be consulted. We were moving and before I knew it, I was celebrating my tenth birthday in Queensland. My tenth birthday and our move interstate would be the start of a whole new life for me, the start of something that would shape me forever.

With so many photos, so much evidence of the beautiful childhood I had, it is unnerving to say that in many ways that I don't recognise that girl in the photos. I don't recognise Caroline the child. I don't know if I would recognise her if I saw her at a local park. Yes, I've seen many photos of her to know her face, though if I heard her voice or read her diary of her hopes and dreams, would I know they belonged to her? That they belonged to me?

What I do know, however, is that I feel the urgent need to rescue her, and at times to hold her by the shoulders, looking her square in the eyes and alert her to what is coming next. I want to warn her of the risk to her innocence. Did she ignore her instincts? Was there anything she could have done differently? My mature adult brain knows the answers to these questions as I've spent a lifetime telling myself that what was to come next was not my fault.

I know as an adult and also now as a parent that this would not be how I would warn my younger self. I would do more to protect her in the first place. As a child I was not equipped with the skills to protect myself and the burden of words of warning would have likely confused me further, and potentially created an even bigger problem and more scars for me to carry throughout my lifetime.

If I ever had that moment though, to sit and speak with my childhood self, would I waste it by warning her and filling her brain with the doom and gloom of what was to come? Or would I simply assure her that she is loved and that she belongs?

I know for sure that I would tell her to remember, that even on the darkest days ahead, that one day, everything will be ok. That even though her hopes and dreams would become foggy as the thickness of the trauma clouded her lived experiences, she would find a way to be a survivor, even as the trauma created a darkness around her memories. I would tell her that one day, people would interview her, that they would ask her about her childhood and she would have an opportunity to look back and know that everything she has done and that everything she will do is exactly what she needs to do. I would reassure her that one day she will be incredibly proud of the woman she will become.

Two

THE BEGINNING

Have you heard of the concept around trauma that talks about the big "T" and little "t"? This theory guides us in understanding that not all trauma is created equal in the lived experiences of human beings. When people remember about trauma, they tend to think about the intense experiences of war, natural disasters, physical or sexual abuse, terrorism or tragic accidents. However, as we know, trauma is complex. It lives with us in our day to day lives on a spectrum based on the details of the trauma itself as well as the impact it has on the people involved.

This big "T" trauma and little "t" trauma concept didn't really make much sense to me until I became a parent. How I choose to parent my sons, how I choose to speak to them and the interactions we have could cause little "t" trauma. This could be in the way that I snapped at them when I was stressed or tired, the way I was not as physically affectionate as I had hoped I would be as a mother or simply how much pressure I put on my sons to do their chores. All of these situations could cause little "t" trauma. This is the kind of trauma that may cause my sons stress, cause them to act in a certain way when put in similar situations and maybe the kind of trauma that would repeat itself one day if they chose to become a parent themselves in the future.

Big "T" trauma, on the other hand, I understood from a very early age. This is the kind of trauma that we read about; the damage that can be caused by violent attacks, significant neglect or surviving extreme environments like warfare. It's the kind of trauma we read about, see on the news, or that people make movies about to help us better understand the human lived experience and the things that we can withstand, but which can cause us significant, irreversible, long-term psychological damage.

The type of big "T" trauma that happened to me, when at the age of 10 my father started sexually abusing me.

Childhood sexual abuse is one of the common big "T" traumas that therapists and psychologists see in their patients. Eleven percent of women and five percent of men in Australia report having been sexually abused before the age of 15. The statistics show us that childhood sexual abuse also comes with a barrage of difficult questions. We bend our brains trying to understand how an adult can choose to use their power to cause harm to a child in this way. How they can ignore the innocence of a child and their fragility, or in some cases actually see that innocence as an opportunity to take advantage of the child for their own gain. Our brains bend almost to the point of breaking when we add the fact that the abuser may also be a biological family member of the child, a person that is meant to have the child's safety as their number one priority. Looking at the data, however, we know statistically that female victims and survivors are most commonly abused by another male relative (35.1%) or by their father or stepfather (16.5%).

The questions around childhood sexual abuse exist in a way to help us understand the scale of the abuse, the physicality of the details and how to act accordingly. These questions exist not only to help us understand the information within the disclosure of the abuse but also to help us work out what to do next. These questions come to us as reactions, sometimes in what seems like a simple moment after a survivor discloses their abuse, questions that form almost immediately as a reactive by-product of the disclosure, placed on the tip of our tongues. The moment we speak our first question the others will ultimately flow, like a tsunami. They are drawn inwards in the gasp as we hear the truth for the first time and are expelled outwards in the waves of questions that come next.

There are so many questions. The most common questions that most survivors will hear are the reactive ones. What did you do? What did he do? What did he ask you to do? How long did this occur? Where did this occur? Did you ask him to stop? Why didn't you tell me? So on and so forth.

So many questions.

So many questions, questions that create a wave which frequently overwhelms the survivor. Some of these questions may be going through your mind now as you try to understand what went wrong in my story, as you try to understand why my father abused me and what our family situation was like for this to occur. We as humans want to make sense of things as quickly as possible, in order to make peace with the disruption that happens in our brains and the flood of emotion in our hearts when we try to process another person's trauma. My story is not about the finer details of the abuse, and I am not here to answer any questions about my experience and what happened to me during those moments where only myself and my father were present. I do not care to share the physical details of each and every moment as it does not serve me to relive the trauma, nor to have anyone relive it with me. I do not believe there is anything to gain by discussing these facts. They are only one piece of this very complicated puzzle.

We assume that these questions will help us, because we want to make sense of the world. In the world where, in my case, my father could abuse me for almost four years. The world where my mother and siblings were not aware of the abuse. The world where I appeared to be a normal child. The world where he appeared to be a normal man. The world where today, I am an accomplished, grown woman with this darkness in my past. We grapple to make sense of that world.

These normalities are true for so many survivors; I've met them time and time again. They walk amongst us, living their normal lives, finding ways to appear as though everything is ok, finding ways to thrive despite their pain. For each survivor walking amongst us, there is also an abuser walking amongst us, masquerading as normal. Both the survivor and the abuser can be ticking time bombs, as Bessel van der Kolk describes in *The Body Keeps the Score*, "Long after a traumatic experience is over, it may be reactivated at the slightest hint of danger and mobilise disturbed brain circuits to secrete massive amounts of stress hormones."

These stress hormones can create unpleasant emotions and intense physical reactions, resulting in impulsive and aggressive behaviour, impacting both the people around the survivor and the survivor themselves.

In my opinion, the answers to the barrage of questions in some ways are pointless. Regardless of the incident, regardless of how long ago it occurred, how frequent the abuse was, the relationship the abuser had with the survivor, and the subtlety or the severity of the actions themselves, *abuse is abuse*. It does not matter if the abuse had been one kiss or if the physicality meant the abuse took the form of violent aggressive rape. The importance lies in the impact it has on the survivor and how it changed them. How it changed me.

For me, the change came in how I turned inward, how I came to rely only on myself and how I lived in the depths of my isolation. In many ways I was living in two worlds and in one of those I was feeling alone, unsafe and vulnerable. I was already the girl who had identified how much I wanted to belong. After moving from another country to a place where I did not speak the language and had to adapt quickly to fit in, belonging had already become a key part of my survival. This compounded further when my family moved interstate, away from our larger extended family, and I once again needed to find a place to belong and a sense of safety and inclusion. I was clutching so hard at a sense of normality in my day-to-day life, whilst this other life was beginning all on its own. I was a child; I had no control. I could not make it stop and it was happening, sometimes daily, parallel to my normal life.

Isolation in one world while being surrounded by people in the other world is confusing, although that leap from one world to another is a skill that survivors of abuse can master quickly after their abuse commences. The leap seems effortless to the untrained eye but it comes with symptoms that can be masked by childish behaviour and the unpredictability of adolescence. In my case, as the abuse occurred for years, I became practised at leaping from one world to the other, switching roles from the young girl in survival mode to the daughter, sister and friend that everyone believed me to be. The good girl I was meant to be.

To the outsider, everything looked standard, with no cause for questions or alarm. I went to school, spent time with my friends, tried new extracurricular activities. I was a good student, participated in everything I was expected to, I wasn't shy or overly extroverted, just nicely in the middle, as normal as can be. My childhood went on for me, all while I continued to go home to an unsafe environment, going home to the unknown of what would come next. Carrying the shame and weight of leaping and living and surviving between my two worlds.

My worlds were so close to colliding, but they never did. Friends would come to visit, but the abuse did not stop. It would continue to happen in the split seconds where my father and I were alone, then someone would walk into the room, missing what had been happening by a fraction of a second as the abuse stopped, just in time for no one to ever see. These worlds were so close, though never close enough to expose the ugly secret, as my mother, siblings and friends never knew what was happening. For them, I continued to be normal, continued to be the daughter, the sister and the friend they had always known. I often wonder if they saw a change in me, if they noticed how hard I must have been trying to be normal. Or if it was simply disregarded as a shift in me and put down to childhood changes. I'm a middle child, easily lost in the space between the older son and the baby girl. I guess I'll never really know what they saw or thought, as that point in time seems like lifetimes ago, a world so far behind the woman I am today.

The real challenge in living this double life was the confusion of it all, the confusion of why this was happening and why it was happening to me. The confusion of how no one saw what was happening right under their noses and the confusion of why I didn't say anything when I was surrounded by people. I grew up in a time where we didn't speak about abuse in school. There wasn't a lot of education around childhood sexual abuse and as we were so far removed from my other family members I really didn't feel as though I had anyone safe I could confide in about what was happening. My instincts were already telling me that the behaviour wasn't right, that what was happening was not meant to be happening. I knew this because my body froze in those moments, it panicked and was conflicted.

Flight, fight or freeze. Flight - where would I go? This was my home, often in my very own bedroom where the abuse would occur most of the time. Fight - he is my father, I was not programmed to fight him, I was to obey as his daughter. Freeze remained the only option; numb the anger, pain and betrayal and box up the memory as soon as possible.

He was my father, my protector, my hero. So why were his actions causing all of these negative emotions, some of which I had never experienced before? Disgust, shame, and deep fear that I had never known before, all created by someone I loved and trusted.

This feeling of shame was why I believe I didn't say anything at the time, why I continued my existence between my two worlds, leaping in and out of them when I couldn't hide in the middle of them. I continued to be as normal as I could for my mother and my siblings. I was never asked by my father not to say anything, I was never directly asked to keep a secret or threatened with any form of harm. These moments occurred, not much was said and then they were over. I did wish that someone would say something, see something, speak up about what I could feel was not normal, what I knew in the depths of my core was not right and what I knew was causing me significant damage. That did not happen and I continued to balance my way through my life and started putting small practices in place to protect myself whenever I could. Changes in my behaviour were so slight no one would see them, but I knew they were there; they were the little building blocks of the walls I was beginning to build to protect myself.

These began in the night, as I changed the way I slept. If you've seen a young child sleep, you'll know that many of them sleep like mini-tornadoes. Children move in the night, sleeping in various positions as their bodies are free to dream and find comfort in the peace that comes from a good night's sleep. This was not how I slept once the abuse began. I taught myself to sleep with the front of my body pressed against the mattress, with my arms pressed against my sides rigidly in an attempt to protect myself like a fortress. I would lie there like a statue as my fingertips would grasp at the blankets creating a snug cocoon around my body, the tips of my fingers clinging tightly to the blanket throughout the night. This was not ideal for a good night's sleep as my body perspired, battling with the heat and relentless humidity of the Queensland nights whilst I desperately attempted to protect myself within my cocoon.

In these moments I lost my innocence, I began to lose my childhood one moment at a time, whilst building walls to protect what little remained of the soft centre of my inner child. At times I was angry at that innocence. Why did it exist in the first place? Why couldn't I be stronger? Why didn't I stand up for myself? Where had my voice gone? Why didn't I say no? Why didn't I flee or fight when I knew what was happening was wrong? Why did I freeze? In those moments of inner conflict, I was broken, wanting desperately to just be a child, to feel safe and to feel free, but knowing that every day I needed to lose the naivety of my innocence so I could be that little bit stronger, so I could protect myself. I told myself that innocence was risky, that I needed to stop being soft, stop being so vulnerable.

I began to build my walls from the age of 10. Those walls were so tall and strong and caused me so much exhaustion as I fought to hold them up for years to come.

Eventually, I found my voice. I spoke up, I asked him to stop, and he did. Unfortunately this was not the end of the freeze, but it was a rare, inexplicable split-second moment where I found my voice. The freeze had done its damage and the effects would show themselves for years to come.

At this moment, when the physical abuse itself stopped, what had been a fear for me for years in some ways was all over. Nothing more was said, the abuse simply stopped and life went on.

These four years had started something in me, the need to build walls, the need to only rely on myself, to keep secrets and to protect myself and in many ways protect my father and our family. The sense of fear that I could only belong to myself and that no one was coming to rescue me, that I had to be my own saviour and that it was me against the world. The sense of shame that these terrible things had happened to me, to my body, and that I had let them happen because I had not been able to ask for it to stop. Because I had frozen.

I did not tell anyone in full detail about what had gone on for those four years. I shared some small details with teenage friends but asked them not to say or do anything. I didn't tell my mother or my siblings; my younger sister was only 6 years old when the abuse stopped and I was so desperate to continue my normal life. To find some kind of harmony and peace between my two worlds. To find a new version of myself where I could blend these two versions of the different girls I had switched between for over four years. To simply get on with life was the goal, as I already knew how much I had missed.

I wanted to create a new chapter, but little did I know how much damage had already been done. This point in my life would one day define my life's purpose in a way, though I had no idea what would come next.

This was the beginning, what would be the first chapter of my story. There were more walls to come, more isolation and so much more pain. Life went on, and I experienced the little "t" traumas of not doing well on a test or of being punished for breaking a rule at home. Meanwhile, the poison of the big "T" trauma was growing under the surface and had already cemented itself as something that would shift my very existence forever.

Three

COMPOUNDING
THE TRAUMA

Teenage girls are complicated. They are fuelled by hormones and their desperate need to find clarity in the space between childhood and womanhood. As their bodies grow, they are quickly thrust into the world of being a woman before their brains are ready to catch up. They walk in a world where they are exposed to so much in the media that tells them how valuable their youthful yet womanly looks are. They are told that they can be womanly and sexy, even when they are still children. They are commodified and taught that their value is visual. That their currency is their face and their body and that they are valued by how appealing these assets can be to the male gaze. That experience was no different for me. I was very tall from a young age and I was acutely aware of the male gaze before I even entered my teenage years, though at the time I had not considered that this awareness was likely a result of the sexual abuse.

My body decided I was a woman well before my brain had even come to terms with what that meant. I had my first menstrual cycle early, well before I started high school so that also seemed to accelerate this path of wanting to be older than what I was. My body simply wanted to be something that my mind in many ways was not ready for; to be a woman, to own my body and what it could do.

I now have a greater understanding of trauma and how it has impacted my body. The trauma shows itself sometimes daily, in my triggers to touch and intimacy, as well as the lasting impacts it has had on my overall health and wellbeing. So, it was not surprising to me to read the 1987 study by Frank Putnam and Penelope Trickett on the impacts of sexual abuse on female development. This study followed 84 girls as they matured to examine how sexual abuse might influence their school performance, peer relationships and self-concept. Putnam and Trickett also looked at changes over time in these subjects' stress hormones, reproductive hormones, immune function and other physiological measures.

The results were unambiguous. Compared with girls of the same age, race and social circumstance, sexually abused girls suffered from a large range of profoundly negative effects including cognitive deficits, depression and troubled sexual development. They also showed abnormalities in their stress hormone responses, had earlier onset of puberty, and accumulated a host of different, seemingly unrelated, psychiatric diagnoses.

In my experience, I craved the attention of boys and young men. It gave me a sense of power. I was desperate for my first kiss with a boy, to please him and in turn to be validated that I was attractive, that I was desirable, that I was worthy of his attention. Somewhere deep inside I almost needed this validation to counter the confusion of the abuse. I needed to know that boys my age would like me and that I was normal. As I became more aware of my sexuality, I found myself craving the attention of older boys and young men. I remember being pre-teen and being mistaken for 17. I lapped that up, wearing it as a badge of honour that boys who were 16 or 17 could be attracted to me, a 12-year-old. I can't even imagine how many times I shared that story as a young teenager, how many times I told the tale of how I had in some way duped these boys into thinking I was almost a woman. I was pleased that older boys could have a crush on me, that even though I was still a child I was obviously much more than a child, because look at what I could do, look at what my body could do and the attention of which it could be worthy.

This double-edged sword of owning what my body could do was also dangerous. I used that façade to my advantage, knowing I could enhance the image of myself to be more than what I really was, to be older, more mature, more of a woman. Yes, I dated boys my age, if you could call it dating - teenage relationships are a curious thing, a rite of passage really. This stage of what in the '90s I called 'going out with' was a fun stage and from what I remember the boys I had as boyfriends were lovely. There were some heartbreaks and some teenage drama but all in all, everything was pretty normal at that point in my life. The boys my age were just as nervous as I was, just as immature and just like me, they were trying to figure it all out.

During this time, I experimented with the concept of truth. I told many lies - some I told to myself to cover up the ugliness of my double life and the world I had to go home to, where the abuse continued to occur. Some I simply told in the hopes of gaining attention from boys and friends, hoping that if they believed the ridiculous stories I was making up, then maybe one day I could tell them the real truth about my life and they would also believe that story. The awful truth seemed so surreal that I wasn't sure if anyone would ever believe me.

The abuse had shifted something in me. It had changed my understanding of relationships and the dynamics of power when it came to significant age differences between two individuals. I was drawn to older boys and young men, and at 15 I found myself in a relationship with a man, who was at the time 24 years old.

I'm not sure what my parents really thought of this relationship; from memory they didn't really push back too much. At this point in my life, I had begun working a casual job, I was doing ok in school and had really emphasised my need for independence. I still carried the bubbling anger and resentment from my childhood abuse as a secret, a poison deep inside fuelled with raging teenage hormonal angst, which meant that I would have argued my point and simply yet defiantly done what I wished to do behind their backs if they had tried to stop me. Yes, I became that kind of teenager, incredibly argumentative and determined to get whatever I wanted, no matter the consequence.

This relationship with this older man went on, and in many ways, it was a fairly normal relationship. As he was older, he drove and we went on dates, spending time together in the evenings and on weekends around my school and work commitments. He met my parents many times and came to family dinners.

Soon after my 16th birthday, I lost my virginity to that man.

Looking back, I can see all of the alarm bells. What kind of man has a relationship with a 15-year-old girl? Did that man strategically wait until I was 16 to have sex with me, knowing that legally if I had been any younger, it would have been a criminal offence? Maybe. Looking back on that relationship there are some glaring concerns, though I can honestly say that I loved that man. I felt safe when I was with him and losing my virginity was a wonderful, loving, consensual experience. Was I a survivor of trauma looking for an older male in my life to love me? Likely, yes. Do I now believe that my relationship with a man who was an adult when I was a child was problematic? Also, yes. Would I do anything differently, looking back? I really don't know. Those years were formative for me and exploring relationships with older men and creating friendships with this new group of people led to a pivotal moment in my life, a pivotal discussion that I would one day see as the beginning of the compounding of the trauma.

What I do know is that at the end of that short-lived relationship, I had a broken heart and a hole of loneliness to fill. A hole that somewhere in my subconscious I decided I needed to fill with a man, another man who was significantly older than I was.

This in itself became problematic behaviour, though I continued to seek the attention of boys my own age, I also sought attention from men, which found me one day arguing with my mother, wanting to take a day trip with a man I barely knew to a remote location, hours from our home. 'It's just a date!' I yelled at her through my teenage-fuelled defiance and anger.

My father was away overseas at the time and she was adamantly telling me that going on a day trip, to a remote location with a grown man that she had never met and that I hardly knew was unsafe and that she would not let me go. 'Think of the things that could happen to you!' she said. 'Think of how dangerous this is!' she pleaded with me. In a moment of white-hot rage, I threw a grenade of words that had the potential to blow up our entire world. In a moment where all I could see was anger, the words catapulted out of my mouth to land at her feet, as the two worlds I had been leaping between collided and then came crashing down around us.

'Why do you care what happens to me? Terrible things have happened to me here, in this house!' I screamed. Each individual word exploded like another grenade, bashing the two worlds against each other, over and over again.

'What terrible things?' she asked. 'Who does terrible things to you?' She was so confused. She honestly did not know anything had happened or what I was talking about.

'Dad does; he does terrible things to me, so don't tell me some man out there is going to do something worse than that!' I screamed back at her. I was too blinded by my rage to see her hurt and confusion. Too lost in the moment to realise how much destruction my words were causing to the two separate worlds I had protected for so long. Those words felt like fire streaming out of my mouth, like the power of a flame thrower hurtling straight for my pint-sized, middle-aged mother. This unsuspecting bystander had no idea what I was talking about and why I was so full of rage.

Tick. Tick. Boom. The grenade hit its target. The flames made contact with my mother and there was no going back. No catching the words and bundling them up to send them back to the depths of the poisonous place where they had escaped from. Back to the darkness of my insides where the trauma and shame lived. I chose a moment of anger and had gone right in for the kill, ready to cause maximum pain and suffering. I do not remember if they are the exact words that were spoken that day. I do not remember what I said next, what she said next, if I continued to yell or if I was crying or if it was a bit of both. I do not recall anything. To me, that moment was like the moment in a Hollywood-style war movie, when a grenade is detonated and you watch it for a moment as it flies across the scene in slow-motion to its destination. The person who throws it knows what is coming, they are bracing for impact as they know what they have done. Everyone who sees the grenade flying through the air knows what is coming. Even though the grenade harms the one person it was thrown at when it explodes, it cannot help but destroy everything in its path.

What comes next can be worse than the explosion itself. The ear-piercing, ringing noise, that moment of aftermath, almost of blackout, as the brains and bodies of the people who are exposed to the grenade assess the scene. It is utter carnage and destruction as everyone attempts to recalibrate and centre themselves again.

What just happened? Why can't I hear anything? Where am I? Did more words come out? I really do not know. It's all blank to me.

There is a vital moment here. A key in the action of what comes next in this echo of white noise. Are the survivors saved and tended to? Or are they left in the rubble to fend for themselves?

In the following days the echoes of the explosion would continue. The grenade's damage and the list of casualties would begin to take shape. There would be a real truth and shaping of character in the moments to come. My older brother would find out about the abuse. Once again, it is all a bit blank to me. I cannot recall if I told him, I cannot recall if I was yelling or if he overheard the argument with my mother. I have no idea. The detonation destroyed the world of those two people that day. Destroyed their relationship with not only their husband and their father but their relationships with me, their daughter and sister respectively. Similar to how I've never been the same since the abuse began, we have never been the same since that moment in time, since I disclosed to them what had happened to me.

Sometimes, I wish I could remember more of the details of those few days. I wish I could remember exactly what I said. I wish I understood why I chose that argument about going out with a man for the day to be the critical moment I told my mother of the abuse. I wish I had more sophisticated language, clearer words, less anger. I wish I could go back and communicate with less emotion and more facts. I wish I could remember what my brother and I talked about, or if we even talked at all. I wish this because maybe if I remembered the details, it would help me to understand what would come next. Why things in some way could go from bad to worse. I believe there is a reason my brain has decided to hide that information away from me; my brain has likely protected me from the beginning of the compounded trauma, because it knows there is little I could have said or done to change what would happen next. Like the soldier in the movie with the grenade, who now has post-traumatic stress disorder, (PTSD) my brain had a blackout at that moment. The blackout is there to protect me in a way, so I do not over-analyse the moment or try to change it. Even now, trying to step back into that moment in time, my ears feel hot, like they are ringing, unable to really tune into the words. My brain protects me from feeling the rage and pain of that moment in time, from reliving the unbearable trauma.

What I do remember is that soon after this moment in time my brother moved out. I was 16 years old, my sister was eight years old; my father was due back from his overseas trip and other than my brother leaving, nothing really seemed to be changing.

I was sent to see a psychologist. A middle-aged man who was lovely from my memories of him, who convinced me after a few sessions that I was fixed and that *my problems* were now gone. Knowing what I know now about psychology and trauma therapy it is clear how problematic it was to send me to this specific psychologist; a man of a similar age, status and power as my abuser. This dubious decision was further compounded when little follow up was made when I decided I no longer wanted to continue with the sessions.

I do not recall ever asking my mother to take us away, I do not even recall thinking that I should ask. Yet as the days went on it became more and more apparent to me that we were not going anywhere. Other than my appointments with my new psychologist, life was going on as normal. Day after day we continued on, no bags were packed, not many questions were asked and we were simply there. In the same home, in the same family setting. The two worlds were repaired, carefully pushed apart, and though my mother and brother now knew that both worlds existed there was an unspoken expectation that I would continue to leap between the two of them.

My mother asked me two specific questions when I disclosed that my father had abused me. These questions specifically related to his penis and my vagina. They did not cover any other form of touching or unacceptable behaviour. They did not open the discussion for me to clarify to my mother precisely what my father had been doing to me and how it had progressed over the four years that the abuse had occurred.

These two questions were limited and my answer to these specific questions was 'no'. This is where the physicality and the scale of trauma become problematic. With these two specific questions the severity of the abuse I had experienced was quickly assessed and the level of trauma was deemed to be minor. No further questions were asked of me. Measures were put in place to fix what was seen as *my problems* in the way of psychological support. Technically, I acknowledge that the abuse was not entirely dismissed or ignored, though looking back now, the impact of the trauma and the impact of the actions to come were not entirely acknowledged or understood.

So that was it; nothing more had to be done. The abuse had a scale, and in this case, any transgressions below these physical violations on the scale was not deemed high enough to warrant ending a marriage or breaking up a family.

I want to be clear here; the sharing of this point in my life and how things occurred is my view of that moment in time. I do not believe the array of questions when it comes to abuse or even the scale of the physical crossing of boundaries is in any way relevant. It is about impact. In this case the impact on my life when I disclosed to my mother that my father had sexually abused me and the second impact when she chose to send me to a psychologist to seek support, whilst also choosing to keep my sister and I in our family home, with our father, while she remained married to him. These actions and choices have and will continue to have a significant impact on my life.

I have only in my adult life become familiar with the word *complicity*. This describes the condition of being involved with others in an activity that is unlawful or morally wrong. Complicity also includes doing nothing or not preventing wrongdoing that is occurring. Another form of complicity is disingenuously choosing to believe that the abuse, once brought to light, would not happen again. This word did not mean much to me as a child, or even as a teenager. If someone had explained this word when I was 16, I would have agreed it was accurate, although I could not in any way have understood the enormity of the impact of my mother's complicity.

I love my mother. She and my father provided me with a loving home where, in many ways, I did not want for anything. Yet, as we have now established, I wanted for the safety, belonging, innocence and freedom that I was robbed of in my childhood. Whilst these things are true, there is still so much wisdom and beauty in my early years. More than one thing can be true, even in the lived experience and my existence as a child.

My mother can love me, want the best for me, want to look after my mental health and seek support for me. She can also continue to stay married to the man who has abused her daughter, she can fail to ask more searching questions, she can put her marriage and the love for and dedication to her husband above her responsibilities as a mother, she can be complicit in his behaviour and the manipulation of a family weakened by his power. She can be more than one thing.

So, we stayed. Our family unit remained whole. In a moment where I could have stopped living a double life, leaping between two worlds, I reached out for a hand, begging for rescue. No one was there. No one took my outstretched hand and pulled me out of the darkness. I was sent back there, knowing that to keep the two worlds alive I had to be sacrificed. I was alone, again. More walls needed building and it was becoming obvious to me that there was someone else to protect now. My little sister, who was 8 years old.

If we were not leaving, if things were to remain the same, how would I know she would be safe? How could I trust my mother to protect her when she had chosen not to take us away? I knew how easily he had got away with his behaviour towards me, though now that I had spoken up and little to nothing had happened, who was going to ensure the same thing did not happen to my little sister?

I was.

Four

THE END OF MY CHILDHOOD, THE START OF CONTROL

When does childhood end? Is it when we are seen as adults in the eyes of the law? Is it when we enter our teenage years and wade through the confusing time between our childhood and our adulthood? Or is it when innocence is lost, when the freedom of childish behaviour is overrun by the need to be safe, by the need to be in control?

My childhood ended when I was 10, when the abuse started. At the very least, a sizeable part of it was taken from me. There was a spark in me that was extinguished when the abuse commenced that I don't think I can ever rediscover. My spark was replaced by a poison that grew into a bubbling, toxic mess, eating away at me from the inside. Though the real end of my era of childhood was at 16, when I disclosed the abuse to my mother, yet we remained in our family unit, living in our home. There is no sense of betrayal quite like betraying yourself. I chose to stay in our family unit, choosing to belong to something that in so many ways did not seem right, but it was the only world that I knew. Looking back, I realise that I wasn't given a choice. I do not recall the decision to stay or leave being one we openly discussed. So, my instinct to belong kicked in, in lieu of any alternatives.

Like many things I have shared so far, I do not recall the exact moments of choosing to stay. I am not sure if I could even call it a choice. Realistically, where would I have gone? With no family nearby there were minimal options available to me. I do not think it really crossed my mind that I could leave and move out of home; I was 16 and still in school. No-one I knew had ever moved out of home as a teenager, it seemed like something only troubled teens did and did not believe that I was a troubled teen. I was a strong, independent young woman but I was not one of 'those' girls. I worked out very quickly that I did not want the labels of being troubled or dramatic. The kind of girls I saw in television shows or read about in books that had terrible things happen to them, who went on to do terrible things to other people, to their own bodies and make terrible decisions that impacted their lives and the lives of the people around them.

The shame would become my silencer, the enabler to keep the secrets I was carrying deep inside of myself. I did not want to be seen as 'other' and did not want the judgement and attention that I assumed moving out of home would bring. I wanted to be strong, to be in control. Not just for myself, but to protect my sister.

That strength was tested throughout my teenage years. Whilst I remained in our family home, now being the eldest child living at home as my brother had moved out, I took it upon myself to be my sisters' keeper. I balanced my teenage life with school, my casual job, socialising with friends and experimenting with life as a whole. However, my sister's safety and wellbeing remained at the front and centre of my focus. I continued to look out for her.

I did not say a word to my sister about the abuse, I did not disclose it to her. Instead I chose to take on the task of protecting her. Her carefree childhood and innocence remained and I kept a close eye on her as the days and years went by. I would go on to stay in this role as her protector for years to come and I would keep the secret from her for the next two decades.

My wish was that asking my father to stop his abuse would give him awareness of his behaviour and actions. I hoped that, by extension, he understood that it was not to occur with my sister either. I hoped he could see the trauma that his behaviour had caused me, how inappropriate his actions were and that none of this was to happen to my sister.

Even still, I remember some nights not wanting to sleep, listening for doors opening or footsteps from one bedroom to another, listening intently for my father and hoping I would not hear him walking towards my sister's room. I can safely say that I did not hear those footsteps.

I don't know if my mother had also had conversations with my father, though I had hoped that she did. I do recall that if my sister was not with me, she was with our mother. Always tethered to one of us, innocently kept by our sides, none the wiser to how hyper-vigilant we had become for her safety.

Sleeping like a baby. Sleeping Beauty. Beauty Sleep. They are expressions that have always seemed foreign to me because even the changes to something as innocuous and innocent as sleep are markers of how my childhood was ripped away from me. Control comes in many different forms. My sleeping had changed since the abuse had started and even when it ceased, I continued to be on high alert, sleeping lightly, hearing each and every noise in our house. It is obvious to me now that this level of stress and hypervigilance was also caused by the fact that I was still living in the house where the abuse had occurred and that I continued to sleep in the same bedroom that I had been abused in for years and years. I also continued to sleep in a tight cocoon with my blankets tucked under myself, flat on my stomach to cover my body, arms pressed against my sides, soldier-like, even in the heat of the Queensland summer. Sometimes, decades later, I still sleep like this. There are days when I am overwhelmed and the triggers are front of mind, and such control feels like a natural and necessary safety mechanism.

When you control yourself, becoming almost robotic, you're building armour to protect what little remains of your innocence and the softer parts of yourself, you don't realise that control can be a double-edged sword.

Controlling myself manifested in choosing to always be that little bit more mature. Not wanting to really let go, show any vulnerability, be silly or carefree or simply act my age. When I restricted myself in those ways to feel that I could be in control of my own safety, I lost the joy of my childhood. The pressure of telling myself that it was up to me, and only me, to make myself safe. That it was up to me to manage my safety and wellbeing and that if something else was to happen to me, it would be my fault. I reasoned that it would be my fault, because I let myself be vulnerable and did not implement the lessons I had already learnt to build more walls and protect myself sufficiently.

During this stage of my life, during the end of my childhood, every moment of heartbreak or disappointment I put back on myself. What a devastating and huge level of responsibility and burden to carry at such a young age! I convinced myself that I was one hundred percent independent when it came to my emotional and physical wellbeing, and that I had to take one hundred percent of the responsibilities and outcomes. It was an all-or-nothing mindset, a me against the world mentality. It was an exhausting and agonising task for a teenage girl to take on, as I doggedly built myself up. Building walls around myself and also turning on myself with criticism and blame, sometimes doing all of these things within seconds of something happening in my life. A vicious cycle of trying to be brave and building myself up, whilst being my own worst enemy and tearing myself down.

This cycle of behaviour caused me to numb myself and to become rigid, closed off from the wonderful emotions that come with sharing a life with others by getting close to people. The emotions that come when having healthy, safe, consensual relationships. I did not realise how much positivity I was numbing from myself and losing each day by seeking such a sense of control. Losing parts of myself, losing my childhood and the pure innocence and simplicity of it.

Numbing to forget, numbing to believe that our family setting could be normal, numbing to believe that my parents loved me, numbing to believe that I could be safe. Attempting to only numb parts of myself but not realising I was numbing it all.

The trauma I had experienced prior to being 16 was only the tip of the iceberg when it comes to what was ahead. It was the beginning of what today feels like a poison. A poison that eats at my brain, taking away pieces of my memory, the pain and the joy, pieces of my life that I may never get back. Every day taking them away from me as my trauma brain fights so hard to forget the hurt, not being able to differentiate the moment, so taking the entire point in time and locking it away. The poison continues to eat away at my memories.

This experience of memory loss is all too common for survivors of any form of trauma. "Memory loss has been reported in people who have experienced natural disasters, accidents, war trauma, kidnapping, torture, concentration camps, and physical and sexual abuse. Total memory loss is most common in childhood sexual abuse, with incidence ranging from 19 percent to 38 percent."

This issue is not particularly controversial: As early as 1980 the Diagnostic and Statistical Manual of Mental Disorder from the American Psychiatric Association (DSM-III) recognised the existence of memory loss for traumatic events in the diagnostic criteria for dissociative amnesia: "an inability to recall important personal information, usually of a traumatic or stressful nature, that is too extensive to be explained by normal forgetfulness."

I was not immune to the impacts of trauma and the ways in which it corroded my memories. It had already begun for me from the age of 10. At 16 I entered the depths of my trauma brain and I have continued to live there ever since. Every day pretending that I was ok. Every day being a daughter, a sister, a friend. Every day being the good girl. Whilst my brain continued to fight for safety, it also continued to attempt to give me a sense of ease and comfort by hiding the trauma. Unfortunately, it unknowingly collected too many other memories along the way, tucking them away out of reach. Not being able to separate the pain and the trauma from the lightness and the joy of life meant my memories were boxed away together.

I have friends who knew me well back then. They share stories with me about moments that we shared together. Stories that I believe to be normal teenage girl adventures. Stories of which I have absolutely no recollection. I relish those moments as they give me glimpses into the memories that I know are stored in my brain somewhere. In those moments with friends, I can have them tell me about myself, tell me about my teenage years and the things we did together. I can experience the memory without having to open the box myself, without having to risk opening up any trauma that may come from that point in time. I can enjoy the delight of reliving the memory, through their stories.

I have a friend who reminds me how I was always looking out for everyone and how patient I was with her younger brother, always making time to play with him when I visited their home. There are so many layers to that story, some are simply parts of me that are still in my personality today. I love children and always connect with them and make time for them when I'm in their company. Though I cannot ignore that my lived experience plays a major role in these moments and why I felt it was important to always look out for everyone, the hypervigilance was not only for my sister and her safety, it was for everyone in my circle.

Sometimes when I hear those stories I almost step outside of myself and for a moment I wonder, who is this Caroline character? It's similar to when I look at photos of my early childhood and smile at the cute little girl who I recognise, because I have looked at those photos so many times, although I still feel as though I do not fully know her.

Feeling as though I do not know myself, or feeling that I do not know myself outside of the abuse forms another depth of my trauma brain. These early years of my life remain suspended in this compounded trauma. These early years of being in our family unit, pretending that I was normal, pretending that my parents were just regular parents. These years were the beginning of what would go on to be the most traumatic years of my life.

The abuse and the trauma are a formative part of who I am and the life that I have lived. I do not know anything else; I did not get to stand at a fork in the road and choose the life I have lived so far. I have done the best I can with the moments in time. I managed to live through and survive the abuse, I managed to go on to live through the trauma which was compounded by remaining in a family unit with the abuser - my father - and my complicit mother. I have survived time after time, while simultaneously being my sister's protector, in many ways putting her needs and the needs of my family and its unity before my own.

In another moment where more than one thing can be true, I can look back at my 16-year-old self and be incredibly proud of her. I'm in awe of her strength, maturity and selflessness. I can also look at her and wonder who she is, wonder what dreams she would have had, if she had been free to dream? I wonder what joy she would have lived if she had not needed to build walls and to wear so many layers of armour.

In a similar way to how I contemplate the existence of Caroline the child, I often wonder, who is teenage Caroline? Would I recognise her today if she passed me in the street? Would she stand out as someone who is no longer a child? Does she look like one of those troubled teenage girls? Or does she look like a young woman, independent and in control? Though similar to my thoughts on Caroline the child, I know that whoever she is, or more to the point, whoever she was, she too will also one day realise that she is a force to be reckoned with.

Five

MY LIFE IN QUARTERS

You may have picked up this book, looked at how many chapters it has and wondered what I might want to share about my life, my experiences and the message I have for you. You may have expected me to dive into more of the details of my childhood, or to have shared more specifics about the abuse itself. So far, we are on a timeline together. I have walked us through the steps of the early part of my childhood in what would seem like a common sequential approach to writing a book about my life.

I want you to understand that because this is a story about my life, that this is a lived experience, an ongoing journey. Throughout this journey, I am experiencing the day-to-day changes that come with being a human being as I process and unpack trauma and how it plays out in my mind and body. This journey is not static, and even as I write these words, I am mindful of how much may change in the days and years to come.

So far, my life in many ways feels like it has been broken up into quarters. There are four significant phases, three of which you are already aware of.

I have shared with you the innocence of my early childhood, the blissful moments before I turned 10. Can you picture the little girl I've talked about? The one that did not speak much English. The one that was surrounded by the love and excitement of growing up in a big family.

Can you see me in my 1980s clothes as I navigate my existence in a new country? Can you feel the giddy excitement I had every time I spent time with my family members, knowing that I could feel safe and loved with them? Can you see the hope and potential of having my whole life ahead of me?

You have then briefly stepped into the shadowy world in the time of the abuse, where there was no escape. Where the trauma began and the vulnerability of my childhood was compromised.

Can you feel the fear of not wanting to sleep at night? Can you feel the tightness in my body as I slept rigid, like a statue, suffocating in the Queensland heat but sacrificing comfort for the perceived safety of my blanket cocoon? Can you hear the door open down the hall? Do you hold your breath like I did, waiting to hear if the footsteps I dreaded are walking towards my room? Does your body tense up like mine as I freeze inside of myself, experiencing fear, shame, disgust and confusion in these moments, night after night?

In some ways, together we have re-experienced the trauma, the parts that I am willing to share with you and we have felt the fear, the heartbreak and the sense of having nowhere to turn.

I have walked you through some of my teenage years, where my trauma brain really started to work its hardest. This is where I established coping mechanisms to survive long-term abuse and emotional neglect. I have shared briefly of my armour, and the walls I had begun to build.

Can you feel how awkward I felt in my body? Can you imagine me looking at myself in the mirror, assessing my beauty and self-worth whilst hating my face and my body, hating what I thought they made men do? Why couldn't my body be something good? Why couldn't it simply be something that existed without it being something that caused so much harm? Can you feel the rage building, compounded by teenage hormones? Can you sense the confusion of trying to understand what was teenage rebellion and what was a cry for help? The emotions of feeling failed by my parents, feeling trapped by the need to have a normal life, the desperation to belong, the sense of blame and guilt that I carried, completely unjustly, all while feeling terribly alone.

These are the first three phases of my life; my life before I was 10, before the abuse. My life in the void that I endured at the time of the abuse, and lastly, my life since disclosing to my mother have been three significant points in time. As I write these words, now in my late thirties, I realise that the third phase, as I moved from adolescence to my life as an adult, has by far been my longest, with the deepest impacts of the trauma.

I am aware these factors of my childhood have propelled me on a journey of self-healing and personal development. They have brought me to where I am today. Brought me to be the woman I am today, the woman who has the language and strength to share her story. But these moments in my childhood are just one part of my story. They are the beginning.

When I chose to stay and to survive amongst the toxicity and the trauma of my family environment, I had to put daily practices in place to protect my physical safety. I had to build my strength by becoming independent and in control of my mental health and wellbeing. When I dived deeper, past the tip of the iceberg of the trauma and continued to live in our family unit, convincing not only the world around me but at times myself that I was normal and that everything was ok, I didn't know how long I would live in a state of fog. I had to take one step forward each day, even when I could not see the path ahead.

I would remain in that fog for 21 years. Fog as a physical element is simply a cloud that touches the ground. It appears when water vapour condenses. You can see fog because of the concentration of tiny water droplets in the air. Similar to this fog, I understood it existed due to the tiny daily droplets of trauma. Depending on the density of the droplets of trauma, their frequency and the traumatic impact they had, the fog at times was so thick it was hard to see through, distorting memories and thoughts for the years to come. I would pretend to be normal and navigate life, even as my memories were numbed and my vision was impaired.

Pretend may not be the right word. Did those 21 years occur? Yes, all while I continued to live my life, exploring the challenges of adulthood and starting a family of my very own. Was that pretend? No. But as I have said, more than one thing can be true. I could be the daughter, the sister, the wife, the mother, the good girl and still be the unknown abuse victim. I could be loved by my parents but neglected by them also. I could be in a happy family with a sense of belonging and miserably lonely all at once. I could live in a place built on rocky foundations.

Foundations are the key to any successful long-lasting structure. They are the first blocks we rely on as they provide the first layer of our structural integrity. In my case, not only were the foundation blocks provided by each of my parents somewhat damaged but what bound them in their pursuit to maintain the normality of our family structure was a poisonous, toxic substance. It kept them together as a combined parenting unit whilst also rotting the entire structure they were building. This substance has gone on to erode each initial foundation block and subsequently, each additional building block added to the structure, from the moment the abuse started and from the moment the terrible truth was kept as our family secret.

In these 21 years from the age of 16, I have actively built my strength and my voice, although there have been many times where everything has come crumbling down. Walls have fallen, mental breakdowns have occurred and I have felt incredibly fragile along the way. In my mid-thirties I realised that I had been building my life on a rocky foundation. I was still trying to build on the damaged foundations of my childhood, hoping that my parents could be the first two foundation blocks to a robust, resilient life. The first two foundation blocks of who I would go on to be. I had been taking elements from each of my parents, to form the core of my existence.

In my mid-thirties I crumbled yet again. I could not build on foundation blocks that were compromised. I had to reframe my thinking, from a place of love, not fear. I had to rebuild. I needed to find the strength to have a voice, to share my experiences and to no longer pretend. Without my parents as the foundation, I would choose to ground myself in myself. Building from a place of integrity, strength, love and accountability. Building as a survivor.

I began building. Piece after piece, identifying the key factors in what was causing damage to my building blocks. The secrets plaguing me, keeping me from my freedom.

This time, instead of building walls, walls that housed my foggy, unhappy memories, I would go on to build an island. A space built from self-love where I could freely enjoy the company of those closest to me in a safe and belonging space. I would create a special place for us, where the people in my life did not have to knock down walls to reach me, where they were welcomed and I was free. A space where the fresh air could shift the fog, where I could feel the sun on my face and experience the freedom to be vulnerable again.

I needed to build my island, I needed to clear the fog. New foundations could not be built on lies and secrets.

So, at the beginning of what I call the fourth phase of my life, just after my 37th birthday I contacted my parents and my brother to tell them I was planning to disclose the abuse to my sister. I needed to start my new life, to live in my truth and I was no longer willing to stay in this hollow place. I was no longer willing to sacrifice myself for something that I believed was not really real.

I was ready for a new chapter, as terrifying as it was to meet with my sister, to sit with her, look her in the eyes and share this truth with her. At the risk of potentially losing her and everything else I had worked so hard to keep, I found the strength to use my voice.

I found the strength to start again.

Six

HOW DID I STAY?

Have you heard of Pandora's Box? It is a phrase that I have personally heard and used many times, not only in my personal life but also in my business.

A shortened version of the story is this; to punish man for accepting the gift of fire which Prometheus stole from the gods, Zeus created a woman named Pandora. She was moulded to look like the beautiful goddess Aphrodite. She received the gifts of wisdom, beauty, kindness, peace, generosity, and health from the gods.

Zeus brought her to Earth to be Epimetheus' wife. Even though Epimetheus' brother, Prometheus, had warned him of Zeus' trickery and told him not to accept gifts from the gods, Epimetheus was too taken with her beauty and wanted to marry her anyway.

As a wedding present, Zeus gave Pandora a box but warned her never to open it. Unfortunately, Pandora, who was created to be intensely curious, couldn't stay away from the box and one day the urge to open the box overcame her. Horrible things flew out of the box, including greed, envy, hatred, pain, disease, hunger, poverty, war, and death. All of life's miseries had been let out into the world. Pandora slammed the lid of the box back down, weeping at what she had unleashed. Then she heard a small voice from inside the box, asking her to open it once more. She relented and found the last thing remaining inside of the box was hope. Ever since, humans have been able to hold onto this hope, in order to survive the wickedness that Pandora had inadvertently let out. The saying "Pandora's Box" now means anything that is best left untouched, for fear of what dreadful things might come out of it.

Stories and analogies have always helped me describe the balance between what is normal on the outside and the unspoken truths that are hidden under the surface. The story of Pandora's Box is one that I use often to share how I've felt for all of these years. My truth has been inside my own Pandora's Box. I have feared opening the box, letting my truth out, as the pain and the death of my illusion of family was lurking inside.

How did I stay? You may be asking this question right now; I know it is one of the questions I often ask myself and it is the question that comes up for many people who have met me or heard my story: *how did I stay?*

There is a raw complexity in the truth of my life, one that I have been exploring in many ways throughout my lifetime so far, so it may even be something I continue to explore for the rest of my life.

I am mindful that one of the key drivers behind this question is a need to understand. For me, it is my need to understand how I withstood the tragic yet beautiful life that I have lived, with multiple truths coexisting. Not only did I withstand the complexity at the time, but have continued to withstand that complexity for over two decades.

The other driver to asking this question is not agreeing with the actions I've taken so far. At times I want more from my past selves and experience a real, deep want to map out a different path. To write a different version of the years to come. To stop the compounded trauma from occurring. I want to stand in front of my 16-year-old self and explain what options she had. I want to support her to do more research, speak to the school, reach out for the safety of trustworthy adults, call on friends and their parents to gain another perspective.

I want her to speak with our mother, to plead with her and to ask her to leave, to pack us up so we could all leave. I would ask her to do something, anything different from the choice she was making to stay in that house with our father. I would support her in exploring the options, in finding the strength to choose being a mother over being a wife. I would help her understand, woman to woman, why her choices need to be different.

I want to sit with my 18-year-old self and help her see how much freedom she already has, that she is stronger than she realises and that if she could find her voice, she could really change things for the better in her world. She could step away from our birth family, and take our sister with her. If she spoke up, spoke to someone with authority, maybe they would let her be the guardian of our sister, maybe they would see that they were both safer away from our father.

These 'I could have – I should have' thoughts can swirl through my mind, sometimes paralysing me with thoughts of the alternative world I could have created for myself, and in turn for my sister. These were not the choices I made. These were not even the choices I felt then or feel now that I had access to. I cannot go back in time; I cannot change the decisions I made and the decisions that were made for me.

I am also mindful that my younger self did not explore these options because somewhere deep down there was an all or nothing mindset at play. Who would choose nothing and dive into the unknown, when you can have it all, even when the all is not whole? Even when the all is broken and toxic, it can be far more appealing than the fear of the unknown and the potential of losing everything.

I think about the choices I made as a teenager, which would subsequently be similar choices that I would make for the following 21 years. I chose family and belonging over safety and freedom. The need to belong came first, and each and every time the foundations crumbled I had to rebuild again.

I chose to live with unspoken truths, to bury secrets deep inside of myself, pretending they were no longer even there feeding the poison, as the toxicity of them bubbled underneath the surface. I chose to put my family first, the illusion of what was coming before myself and before my safety. I chose to belong over every other vital need.

Belonging to a family is something that most of us understand. There is a human desire at the very core of our existence that requires us to belong to something. Choosing to belong to my family meant that in many ways life went on as normal. This in turn reinforced the idea that by choosing to stay in many ways I never felt that I had made the wrong choice.

For over 21 years we all remained in our family setting. I played the part of the daughter and sister that I was meant to be. I played the part of the girl who had overcome the abuse and could remain in her family, where her abuser sat every day at the head of the table. I played the part of the girl who was *ok*, who would go on to be the woman who was *ok*. Everything was going to be *ok*. I would go on to be the woman who convinced myself that if the world did not know then maybe, just maybe, I could be normal and that the ugliness would not haunt me forever.

When I look back over my life so far there are so many moments of belonging and family that have been shared with my family members and the people around us. Looking back on my life, a life that has been real, I sometimes look at those moments and regard myself in some ways to have been a brilliant, award-winning actor. One who played the part so convincingly that not only did I convince the people around me that everything was exactly as it seemed, but that I convinced myself that it was real. The greatest lie, told to myself. Waking up every day to live inside the lie. Hoodwinking myself and having years of evidence to prove that the lie was real, that even though more than one thing can be true, that I could still pick and choose the truths I would believe. The truths I would acknowledge. The truths I would show the world.

There are years and years of these moments I could share with you. A lifetime of evidence of the life I have lived so far, alongside my family members. Smiling, laughing, creating memories and belonging.

One that I remember clearly is graduating high school, and attending my Year Twelve formal. Looking back on those photos I was wearing a powder-blue dress; my hair was curled and my make-up was done by a professional make-up artist. I even had my fingernails manicured and painted for the occasion, which seemed to be a very big deal at the time and emphasised the importance of this milestone event. Now I look back on those photos with horror, though not the horror of what must have been happening to my mental health by balancing the trauma whilst living a somewhat normal life. No, the horror comes with reliving the terrible fashion of looking like a fairy-tale princess, coupled with the ghastly attempts of the make-up artist, who obviously had no idea what to do with brown skin. She evidently thought blue eyeshadow the same colour as my dress was a good idea! I'm amazed by how old I look for a 17-year-old girl, thanks to the fashion, hair and make-up choices of that day. The horror of the early 2000s in all their glory. I laugh even thinking about this day and these photos as they capture such a formative rite of passage. A rite of passage many children experience as they celebrate the success of completing their school years, and one that I was not denied. A rite of passage that I chose, knowing that if I had left home that graduating high school may have been jeopardised. There are photos from that night of me with my family members, there to congratulate me and celebrate this milestone event. These moments are real, they happened, the actor continued to act, further developing the believable fictional character of Caroline, the good girl.

Twenty-one years, however, is an incredibly long time to play a role. I think about some of the long-standing shows that are running on television. The dramas that have characters who have played the same role for decades, sharing hours of their days with their fictional family members. Moving, talking and displaying their emotions 'in character'. Does that actor go home and become someone else? Or do they eventually blend and merge their character into their real selves? Are they one and the same? I think of the actors who have played a role since they were a child. Does it really remain a role or is the fictional character forever embedded in their true self? Are they destined to always be their fictional character?

When is something nonfiction and fiction all at once? I have hard evidence to prove that these moments happened and were some of the happiest moments of my childhood. I have living memories that we as a family came together to share true moments of joy. I also have the values and skills to know that my parents have taught me so many of the things that make me the successful person I am today. As I've grown into an adult there are the photos that show my parents were with me when my first child was born, holding their first grandchild with nothing but love and pride in their eyes. There are photos from the day I was married, with my father walking me down the aisle. There are countless photos of my parents with my eldest son, showing that they played an active role in the first few years of his life. I have all of these photos that prove that we were and could have continued to be perceived as a happy, normal family. They show smiles as we stand bunched in together, posing for the camera. Our similarities and features are shared, reminding the world that we belong together, that these details connect us as a collective, these features show that we are a family. I can read over years of birthday and Christmas cards where I've written highly of my parents, told them how I love them and reminded them of the qualities I admire in them. Written words of thanks, written evidence of a daughter who belonged.

We were normal, commonplace almost. We were just like you and your family.

Over the years I have opened my Pandora's Box slightly, letting out small parts of my story. I have sought out mental health support from professionals. I have educated myself on the impacts of abuse and looked after myself, attempting to improve my wellbeing for myself and for my nuclear family of my husband and children. I have made changes to how I live, not only in my life with my nuclear family, but to the role I play with my birth family and who I share my truth with outside of my family settings.

These have been small moments of sharing my truth with the world, on occasions when the wickedness contained within my Pandora's Box escaped and could be survived in small doses. Small moments when I shared my truth and felt the need to belong to my family faded slightly as the desire to be free became more appealing to me.

For the most part, however, the lid remained firmly closed, and inside of the box my truth also remained hidden. Inside the box remained my freedom and my hope. Just like the greater hope mankind has when it comes to surviving the wickedness of Pandora's Box.

There has always been a fear when it comes to deciding to completely open the box. There are thoughts and fears that working through the pain of what is inside would take years and a strength that I may not have in me. There is a fear of loss and a fear of hurt I may cause to the people I love along the way. There is a fear that I may lose the lid and may never be able to close the box again, exposing myself and the world to never-ending wickedness.

I remind myself that one day the box will close and in that moment of hope, I can find my freedom.

Throughout all of these insights, I am conscious of the judgement that exists around my story. This feeling of judgement from others is something I carry with me even to this day; I know that you may not understand or agree with my actions so far. You may want me to do more, to speak louder. I believe that your judgement is not mine to carry on my journey, and though I hope that your thoughts come from a place of concern for the safety of myself, my sister and any other children in our world, this matter is complex, my family is complex, humanity is complex and my decisions have come from a place of empathy. Empathy towards myself and also my need to belong to something greater than me, at the cost of myself. It has taken time to develop real empathy for the decisions I have made so far and in knowing that I have done the best I could with what I had, and that I have worked at my own pace and in a way that I felt was best for me.

When I revisit the question: *how did I stay?* I'm reminded of the complexity of the abuse and the confusion around it all. I have forever feared the judgement of others at the sheer ugliness of the abuse. Childhood sexual abuse is a horrible act in itself, and I have another layer of horror as the abuser is my father. We often prefer to view perpetrators as the trolls under the bridge that we can keep our children away from, people that we obviously need to protect them from. I can tell you first-hand that the perpetrators do not look like the monstrous troll under the bridge, nor are they the horrible monsters we imagine them to be, all bad, nothing good in them. Nor are the survivors of abuse damaged and broken, weak, leftover shadows of humans that we need to pity. I can show you many examples contrary to these images. I can show you the evidence of my life today that is rich and full, that also involved childhood sexual abuse.

I can show you a life of opportunity and love. The life of a successful woman who stands before the world knowing that I can only make decisions today at this moment on my journey, I can only choose today to do better, because I know better.

I can choose to find the courage to open my Pandora's Box and release my hands' grip on the lid. By telling my story, I am choosing to let everything escape so that I can experience the entirety of everything that lies within the box, knowing that once I find the hope at the very bottom of the box, I will be free.

Seven

THE IMPACT OF STAYING

As a parent, I find myself constantly speaking to my children about impact. I have been acutely aware since they were very little that my actions and decisions impact them, as much as theirs impact me. Having such a lived and intimate understanding and experience of big "T" and little "t" trauma meant I am highly selective in my parenting and how I communicate with my children. As they have grown, I have used very clear and simple language to help them understand the impact that they have on themselves, the world around them and the power of their choices. Their choices not only in what they do but how they feel and how those two elements combine to influence what comes next.

Cause and effect.

I taught my children that when they bounce a ball inside, there is the potential that that ball could bounce out of their control and unintentionally break something. I also teach them about the effect that could come after and the emotions that could form as they felt embarrassed and regretful, in addition to the emotions of frustration and disappointment from myself and their father. A simple example of cause and effect, a lesson taught over and over (and in my case with my youngest child, who is besotted with tennis, over and over and over again!) all around the world.

Emotions play a major part in my message to my children about impact. For many years, I've talked about the common spaces in our home, the living room and dining table. In these communal spaces, my children are reminded that we all share the space together, and that their actions, both physical and emotional, can have an effect on others. Although no one is expected to bury or deflect their emotions or the need to physically move, common spaces need to be shared in a safe and welcoming way. Big emotions and big movements may not be safe for the others around us, so we need to find ways of expressing those in other ways, in other spaces.

This common space, where we talk, move and be, whilst respecting each of the individuals we share the space with is something that I dreamed of as a child. I do not remember this kind of language in my household growing up. Though I grew up in a loving family, I do not recall being told that certain spaces were where we could be free to speak our truths, no matter how big the emotions were around them.

By the time I was 16, there were already some tell-tale signs of the impacts of the abuse I had experienced, which would have been obvious to anyone who was willing to look closely enough. My romantic relationship as a teenage girl with a grown adult man should have been one of the first concerning signs of impact, a clue that something was not as it seemed to be. Surely conversations needed to be had as to why a 16-year-old girl would want to pursue a relationship with a 24-year-old man? The next question is obvious: why were my parents not doing anything to end this relationship and protect their daughter? These sorts of things were clear evidence of the scars underneath the surface.

The impact and effects may have been visible to anyone who knew me back in my teenage years, the teenagers I went to school with or people in my friendship group. Though I am sure in many ways I masked my behaviour under the all-so-common expectations that teenagers are just rebellious and will push boundaries to experiment with life. I was the child who started smoking cigarettes before I even started high school, flaunting my desire to be cool and look older than I was by sometimes even smoking near the gates of my primary school. Looking back, I know that this was a mix of the urge to rebel and to try things I knew I wasn't meant to experiment with. It was also another clear tell-tale sign, another cry for help. As a parent, if one of my children had begun smoking cigarettes before high school, I would be aware that I needed to investigate further, as something was likely to be terribly wrong.

Entering high school, the smoking continued and escalated, combining the use of marijuana and drinking alcohol. I think back to those years and wonder how no one at home ever noticed I was using these substances, though I realise now, if sexual abuse can occur in my childhood home and not be detected, underage drinking, smoking and drug use was just another activity that would fly under the radar. Were they truly oblivious to what was happening right under their noses? Or was the reality too much to face, the choice to ignore being far more blissful than the choice to see the truth for what it was?

At 15 years old, the peak of my teenage years, the years between the abuse ending and disclosing it to my mother, I would smoke cigarettes at school most days, accompanied by an unruly bunch of teenage friends. We would find places to smoke on the school grounds, sometimes even smoking marijuana during the school day.

At my worst, when I had lost all hope and had little to no regard for my body and mental health, let alone my education or reputation as a student, likely at the point my teenage self was the most desperate for some kind of intervention, I began to drink alcohol during the day at school. One particular day I drank so much at lunchtime that I attended my afternoon classes completely intoxicated. I vividly remember sitting at my desk in that hot Queensland classroom as the room was spinning. I desperately tried to keep my head upright, my hand propped under my chin trying to keep myself from either falling asleep or vomiting as the room continued to spin. The smell in that classroom was horrific. With no air conditioning, the combination of my breath, body odour and the sweat of the teenagers around me was putrid.

I cannot even imagine what the other students were thinking, I must have reeked of alcohol, my skinny body trying to expel the liquid as I sweated profusely. There were other students who had been drinking with me that day who were off in their own classrooms, likely experiencing the same torture and hoping just like me that we all would get away with this ridiculous act of rebellion.

To this day I think I would have gotten away with my teenage drinking that day, as my regular teacher was not at school and the substitute did not know me well enough to know how odd my behaviour was, but another student had been found out. We all dreaded what to do as we prepared to face the consequences of our actions over the coming days. We were all doing our best to protect each other and find some kind of common story to save ourselves from the punishments that could come.

This moment is another sliding doors moment for me. Another moment where I feel I was failed by the adults in my life. In the days after I had been drunk at school, I sat in the school office, speaking with the school counsellor and another staff member and explained to them that I was in a fragile and abusive family environment and that if I was to be punished or my parents were to be informed, that it would be detrimental to my safety. I did not share details of the abuse that had occurred in my childhood. At that moment my acting must have been another stellar performance as they believed my story and acknowledged that I was as fragile as I claimed to be. In what I now realise to be a huge error in their duty of care and significant neglect by the school, from my understanding no call was made to my parents. The school did not punish me to any great extent and my disclosure of my unstable, abusive family environment, which was obviously causing poor decisions such as underage drinking, was not investigated. The secret continued to remain hidden in me and I continued to convince the world I was normal. The actor continued to act.

Teenage Caroline was smug. I had dodged the bullet of suspension or even worse, expulsion. My parents acted the same way that day when I came home from school as they did every other day, and I continued to act the same. They did not seem to have any idea of what kind of damage I was doing to my body and my mental health. Life went on, I remained at the school, and took care to not drink so much that the room was spinning! I maintained my lie, that everything was ok.

By the time I graduated from high school I had mastered the art of my acting. It seemed I had proven that despite the toxic secret living inside of me I could go on and live a normal life.

A few years out of high school I met a man who would go on to be my first husband. Another man who was far older than me, this time 12 years older. We would be together for over seven years in what I often describe as a turbulent relationship. Another clear tell-tale sign, another effect of the impact of my childhood abuse, my desperation to be normal and my desire to soothe something in me that was eating away at my insides. Like most things this turbulent relationship was beautiful and tragic all at once. It mirrored what I had already experienced to be family. I lived in a new world that was not perfect but convinced myself that it was. Yes, even in my first marriage life continued to remind me that more than one thing can be true.

Looking back, I can see the signs so clearly, the signs of impact and the decisions made to live through the emotion of it all. The abuse and the choice to live in a family setting with my birth family after disclosing the abuse to my mother has had a significant impact on me. Nevertheless, I do not believe I am any better than any other survivor in hiding the impact. I am no greater actor than the survivor that you may have met in your life, who gets up every day, taking life one day at a time.

We all do this as survivors. We master the art of masking our feelings of betrayal and neglect so we can seek out the more positive emotions and interactions. We hide and bury the hurt so we can focus on the positive and achieve. Sometimes the achievement is simply getting out of bed that day and having a shower. Sometimes the achievement is sitting down to write a memoir of your life and its complexities. Every day is different and every day comes with its own set of challenges and level of impact.

One thing to remember is that impact is all about perspective. We often want to have a one-size-fits-all approach to how survivors are meant to process and live with the trauma of their abuse. Some expect survivors to rebel, to be like teenage Caroline, choosing to numb myself with drugs and alcohol to be able to become the polished actor. Some survivors throw themselves into activism, trying to understand the world and make bigger changes for the better. Some simply just live day by day, walking among us, simply quietly getting on with life. Some do all of those things on any given day, week, month. None of these examples are one-size-fits-all and none are greater or less than each other. They are simply how society chooses to see the impact of abuse and attempts to categorise it for the sake of understanding.

The main challenge I faced throughout the 21 years of living in the normal setting of my birth family was the heaviness of always feeling betrayed.

Being betrayed by my father, when he chose himself over my wellbeing and brought the ugliness of childhood sexual abuse into my life. Betrayed by my mother when she chose herself and her marriage over me and my safety. Betrayed by myself as I pretended that everything was ok, as I continued to put our family unit before myself, the child who had been abused. The heaviness of it all, every single day.

I spent over 21 years sacrificing myself, from the age of 16 until I was a 37-year-old woman, acting out my fictional character to maintain the integrity of all of the characters around me. I see my family and where they reside to be somewhere I refer to as the mainland. In this analogy, the mainland is where I lived since the abuse occurred and where I have spent the majority of my life. My parents live on the mainland and so do my siblings with their families and loved ones. This is a place where they roam freely, free to enjoy the comforts of each other's company, enjoying the safety and love that comes with family.

But the mainland is infested with shame, a place full of explosives. Some are mines, hidden under the surface of the ground. Some are grenades that fly through the air, kicked up by my family members who walk along unharmed, somehow immune to the explosive perils of this place. In my mind, the mainland is a dangerous place. I had to live there for many years, and every birthday or special occasion I had to sacrifice myself and my wellbeing to walk on the mainland knowing that my choice to seek love and belonging could mean stepping on an explosive, and in turn having to nurse myself for weeks after the damaging moment in time. It was a high price to pay, knowing that the fleeting moment of love and belonging would be overshadowed by weeks of recovery.

Sometimes being on the mainland felt normal, and the fictional character I had played for so long told herself that if I stood still for long enough that I might be ok. I could belong in that place, I would not need to step on any explosives, I could stand still and simply be there, to belong. Those would be the days the grenades would be thrown unintentionally and I would suffer the unexpected triggers where a word or the casual touch of a loved one would send me back to the abuse, back to the body-freezing terror of the moments with my father. So even in the stillness of wanting to be on the mainland, wanting to belong, I was still not safe.

Over the years, when I have disclosed the abuse to people, one of the things they have said to me, time and time again, is that it is not my fault. I know this to be true. Not at any stage was I responsible for the sexual abuse or the choices that were made by my parents. Simultaneously, I also know that in some ways I have chosen to be the scapegoat of our family. I have chosen to swallow and survive each and every explosive designed to destroy me. I have martyred myself to save my family, or more specifically, my siblings, from experiencing the destruction of the explosives. The destruction that comes from the truth.

The impact of living in this state of trauma and hypervigilance for over two decades has been incredibly detrimental to my mental health and my relationships with my loved ones. It has meant that I've chosen to numb myself from emotions, for fear of the pain that comes with getting too close and the fear of experiencing vulnerability with my husband and my children. I do not get to pick and choose which emotions I keep and which I remove; they all get packed away together. Similar to the fog, the tiny droplets of trauma cause a distance, a way to not really see the people I love, right there in front of me. In packing away emotions, I also pack away the memories I've made. The fog settles in and my vision diminishes further. It is a numbness that I have lived with for far too long, one that I am letting go of more and more each day.

Today I have created a safe common space that I share with my loved ones. It is one where we can experience emotions and express them, and when they are too big or volatile for the shared space, when we need to step outside, we can do so accompanied by our loved ones so we have the freedom to be big, to feel big, to scream and move with emotion and know that it is part of the impact of life.

I have created something special, and my loved ones know that there is a safety, respect and love expected in this space, but also a freedom that comes from living together, on the secure island I have built for us, far away and safe from the mainland.

Eight

LOVE FOR MY MOTHER

The challenging reality that I have come to face over the past few years is the fractured relationship I have with my mother. There are knots in my stomach when I think about the decisions I have made in recent years, decisions that were and continue to be designed to preserve myself. It is painful to put boundaries in place when you love someone so dearly. I love my mother, ever so much. It is that love that makes the hurt and betrayal so unbearable at times, the yearning to visit her on the mainland, the wish to find a way to be there and to also be safe. That is the love that had me stay in our family setting, on the mainland for so many years.

When I think about the life we have lived together it is filled with so many beautiful memories. Like other moments in my life, I have the photos to show the moments of my early childhood where we ventured to the beach in Mauritius, my mother looking as beautiful as ever as she wrangled my chubby toddler body that was eager to dive into the ocean, splashing in the vivid blue water, sand wedged between my chunky little toes. These photos are colourful, both of us wearing bright swimsuits and sitting on the sand together or wading in the shallows of the ocean. We were always surrounded by the warmth of family, always having additional extended family members sharing these moments and memories with us.

There is a photo I cherish where I am sitting on her lap in the front seat of a car, with my brother standing next to us inside the door of the car. He has a concerned look on his face in all his big brother glory as my mother pretends to give me a sip of a fizzy drink. She likely only lets the bottle touch my lips, creating this moment for the camera to capture. It is one of those moments I cannot remember for myself but one that I have the photos of to hold on to, capturing this hot day in Mauritius where cold fizzy drinks were desired by all, even the chubby toddlers, to the alarm and heartfelt worry of big brothers.

My mother was stunning, I have seen many photos of her in her youth and thought of how striking she was. I should not say she *was* in the past tense, as this beauty did not fade over the years; she is still regarded to be an incredibly beautiful woman. It makes me smile to think of how many people have compared my beauty to hers over the years. I am aware that I have had various opportunities in life offered to me because of my looks and I know that my beauty in many ways comes from her. It makes me proud to have people point out to me how much I look like her, how I have her features, her nose, her eyes, her smile and how lucky I am to have some of her beauty.

I know that she was, from the very beginning, a truly loving mother. There are so many photos of her doting over me, looking lovingly at her baby girl. Eyes full of love, protection and wonder. I have similar photos of myself holding my children when they were babies, that look of adoration is so familiar to me. In many ways that look is universal, a mother's love that knows no bounds and is timeless in its purity.

When I look at my life, from the very beginning there was nothing but love from my early childhood days. My needs were always met and even when my health and body tested me my mother was always there. She has shared with me that at the age of 10 months old I began to be unwell, not being able to hold down food. This vomiting continued and my parents took me to a paediatrician who checked me over, gave me some medication for the vomiting and asked my parents to monitor me.

When the vomiting persisted, my parents took me to the Clinique Mauricienne, the private hospital, and I continued to be treated for gastro symptoms. After two days, with the vomiting still persisting, I began to become pale and showed significant distress as my stomach spasmed and fever began to rise. The medical professionals realised there was a blockage, an X-ray was requested which required a barium meal to be inserted into my stomach via a tube down my throat. I continued to vomit, my tiny 10-month-old body convulsing trying to reject the liquid required to perform the X-Ray. My mother has told me that she was beside herself with worry and thought that I could die that day. The medical professionals persisted as my parents held me down for the X-ray to be performed, my tiny body on a cold medical table, in the dark, sanitised room. My mother wished for it to all be over as she stood and held me still for the procedure.

The X-ray showed that my intestines were completely blocked in a condition that is known as intussusception, a serious condition where a part of the intestine slides into an adjacent part of the intestine. This telescoping action blocks food and liquid from passing through normally and can also cut off blood supply to parts of the intestine. My parents were told that surgery must occur immediately and I was prepared for the operating theatre.

My mother recalls that the operation took two to three hours, though she has shared with me that she does not remember the exact time. She has told me that it felt like an eternity and that she spent the entire time praying that the operation would be a success. After many hours the doctor came out of the operating theatre to tell my parents that the operation had gone well, my intestines were unblocked and that they had also decided to remove my appendix to prevent further issues in the future.

My father went home to tend to my brother, and my mother stayed with me overnight. She lay on a hospital bed as I slept in a cot beside her, though she did not sleep at all throughout the night. This post-operative time was the most critical for my survival. I was running a high fever and the health professionals had concerns that the antibiotics they had administered would be rejected by my body, which would impact my recovery. My mother recalls a nurse coming in to help her remove my sweat-soaked clothes and having to use scissors to cut them off due to my body being covered in medical tubes and bandages.

The sweat-soaked clothes were a good sign though; my fever had begun to subside and I had made it through the night. I was out of danger. My mother called my father to let him know the good news and he came back to the hospital early that morning to see us both.

Once I was out of danger the nurse shared with my mother that she had been very concerned during the night, because most babies do not live after this operation and that we were fortunate that I had survived. I was a survivor already, at 10 months old.

My parents took me home a few days later and I healed quickly. I went on to be that chubby, well-fed toddler, and on from there to be the woman who is told often that I am beautiful, just like my mother.

Telling you this story, this story of my mother's love and the survival of baby Caroline, makes the other parts of my story even more confusing, I know. Yes, it is clear in many ways that a life-or-death medical operation for a 10-month-old baby is when we expect mothers to do their best work. When we expect them to go above and beyond to protect their child and find the answers to reduce and remove the pain. We expect mothers to save their children, we believe this to be an inherent trait that mothers are gifted the moment their children are born. So, when does that change, and when is the pain of a child not great enough to induce sacrificing other elements of life? When did my mother choose to be a wife over choosing to be a mother?

You may be wondering why she has stayed, why she remains married still to this day. I have asked those questions, too. But no answers have changed her actions. She can be more than one thing and she and I can disagree with what we believe to be the right thing to do as a mother.

I have painted a picture for you already, of the stunningly beautiful mother who looked at her child with love. Of the mother who lay beside her baby daughter, praying for her to live through the night after life-saving surgery. I have also painted the picture of the mother who did not see the abuse that was occurring in her own home, abuse caused by the hands of her husband, inflicting harm to her daughter. I have shared with you the mother who did not leave when she found out about the abuse, even when she had another young daughter to care for. I have shared with you the mother who continued to expect her daughter to remain in her family setting, with her abuser, in a family filled with love but carrying a dark secret.

These are only some of the brush strokes I have painted for you when painting the picture of my mother. She is a masterpiece, a whole being, with brush strokes painted before my birth, painted by herself and the people around her. As I paint each brushstroke for the portrait I share with you, I am reminded of the beautiful memories, of all of the lessons I have been taught by my mother. I am reminded of the happiness and joy we have shared and of the various moments we have created together and of the love I have for her.

I am also torn by the push and pull of good and bad. Constantly haunted by the question; what makes us good? I know that more than one thing can be true. I know that my mother can be a good mother, she can help save my life and she can also stay married to an abuser. She can be a good and bad mother all in the same person. If she was to leave him, would that make her good? Or would that simply make her a bad wife, abandoning the man she swore to love until her death? Can she only be good in one role, that of wife or that of mother? Does she have to choose? When she chooses what does she lose in the process?

These questions have slowly eroded my relationship with my mother for many years. They make our relationship feel fake because there are times when I second-guess myself and wonder what is real and what is acting. What is love in its truest, purest form and what is done out of duty, by default? What is the love that is *meant* to be there because of the titles of our relationship, Mother and Daughter?

Being in a relationship with my mother caused me to feel like a fraud in the world of advocates and allies. I would preach, sometimes shouting, about the role that mothers play in protecting our children. I would talk about my mothering, and how I protect my own children and the role I play in their lives. In those moments, surrounded by other parents, fellow survivors of abuse, or even the strangers that have listened to my thoughts through the world of social media and the internet, I have felt like a fraud, living a lie of family and a mother-daughter relationship without really knowing if she was good or bad, without really confronting my own hurt and pain.

Is she good or bad? Can she be both and who decides in the end? Can she be redeemed for her choices, or what may be seen as her mistakes? Can she be a good wife, a good mother to my siblings, a good mother to me in my early childhood and a bad mother to me after my disclosure? Why does she stay with him? What happened to her for her to choose to stay? Why doesn't she choose me? Can I accept that she is more than one thing?

So many questions that will forever go unanswered. They are not my answers to know or to hold. They are hers; they are her truth.

Dear Mum,

I love you; I know that I always have and always will. In so many ways I am forever grateful that you are the woman I get to call Mum. Throughout our life together I have had the pleasure of seeing you shine, in your beauty, in your grace, in your intellect and in your love for me. I have seen you look at me with pride when I have, despite the darkness, gone on to succeed in the many things I have attempted in life.

I know that our distance hurts you, but I also know that somewhere deep down you know why I choose the life I live today and why I will continue to choose it. You have taught me that life is about choice, that we cannot control what the people around us do, but we can choose how we are impacted and what we do next.

I want to thank you for all that you have taught me, as the integrity and strength that I hold today comes from the lessons you have shared with me. They do not all come from hard times, they also come from the examples you have set in many other ways and from the love I have seen you show to others in our lives.

Thank you for loving me, thank you for respecting my boundaries and thank you for being my mother.

I miss you and I hope that you find the peace and harmony you seek in this lifetime. If you choose to, I wish for you to find your island, where you are safe, away from the mainland.

Caroline

x

Nine

HUMAN SACRIFICE

Throughout history, many cultures across the world have practised human sacrifice. We've heard the tales of discovered tombs, some dedicated solely to children, their mummified bodies unearthed by archaeologists. Some of these human bodies can be found interred near the summit of mountains and volcanoes. Some have been found near iconic man-made structures and some, no doubt, will never be found at all. Their stories were carved in stone as a way to honour the sacrifice offered and the life presumed to be gained by the rest of mankind after the sacrifice.

Some of the tales, such as that of the Aztecs, consist of priests slicing into their captive's torsos, removing their still-beating hearts to feed the gods, to ensure the continued existence of the world. Death was only the beginning of the victim's role in the ritual of the sacrifice; priests would carry the bodies to another ritual space, making further incisions to the body, laying the bodies out to the gods as an offering. Eventually over months or sometimes years, in the sun and rain, the remaining skull of the victim would begin to fall to pieces, losing teeth and perhaps even its jaw. The priests would remove the skull to be transformed into a mask, placed as another offering. The skulls were seen as the seeds that would ensure the continued existence of humanity, a sign of life and regeneration. Without this kind of sacrifice, the Aztecs believed that the sun would cease to rise and that the world would end.

For many of us today, cultural rituals like this seem barbaric and callous. Many of us live in cultures and societies that value human life, and though religious and cultural beliefs still remain an important part of our society, in most cases we live in countries that have laws in place prohibiting the death of human beings in this way.

When I think about these tales of sacrifice and how embedded they are in the roots of our history I am not surprised that elements of human sacrifice still exist to this day. When I ask myself, when and how did I learn that it was my job to sacrifice myself and my wellbeing to make the people around me comfortable, I can find the answers to the questions in the depths of our human history. The institutions that we belong to, by choice or by birth, form the structures that we live in. The institution builds the arena, piece by piece and explains clearly, sometimes by words but many times by actions, the rules and regulations that we are expected to play by, to live together in this common space. In this arena, there are the box seats. The people in these seats built the arena to benefit themselves and their beliefs. The rules they created are set to serve themselves and those they believe to be like them, to protect the space they have created, even if the space is based on falsities and fear.

In my sacrifice, the mainland I lived on became the arena. My parents were in the box seats, dictating, many times without words, the human sacrifice I needed to make to uphold the structure of our space. The sacrifice I needed to make to convince the world that everything was ok, that we were normal. The message I received was that the institution and structure of family and its importance far outweighed the value of one life, my life. Rules of moving on past the abuse, staying quiet and still outwardly succeeding in society were unspoken, though behaviours were modelled and expectations were very clear. I showed up, day after day, led by my parents and played the role I was expected to play. I was the good girl, the obedient daughter, the clever girl who would go on to be a successful woman. The actor continued to act, regardless of whether I knew that my role was fictional or if I believed this to be my one true life. I would not speak a word, I would not make a sound, I would continue to follow the rules.

Within my sacrifice, I had named myself many things over the years, given myself ways of trying to cope with the reality of it all, especially since becoming an adult and reflecting on my place in my family. I had dreamt of outside realities, a space away from the mainland, a space of freedom. Sometimes I called myself the black sheep of our family. Explaining to people when they asked about my family and my relationship with family members, I'd say that I was just that little bit different from my other family members. I shared with people my feelings of difference and related that difference to being something simple, something most families experience. This excuse gave me a sense of distance when I didn't want to belong because belonging meant sacrificing. It was a comment that people could grasp easily and understand without me having to share my truth, without me having to explain why I needed to be different. I would use my title of the black sheep and justify the fact that someone in our family had to take on the role of being difficult and different and that for whatever reason that role had fallen on my shoulders. The black sheep could stray from the flock. No one would question that because the black sheep was different to the others. It was not that bad after all, because most families have a black sheep. I took on this title without hesitation, and it continued to be an easy way of deflecting my pain and highlighting the reasons why I did not belong, instead of highlighting the reasons why I was sacrificed. Why I had been the one who was worth less than the others.

Even within my own family, with my siblings, I have used names and alternative stories for myself as a way to create an alternative to my reality. I have wished that I was adopted, openly telling my own siblings that one day we may find out that I did not belong with them. That I had been placed in our family, but that somewhere out there my real family existed. In these moments I was not the mean older sister we see time and time again, who torments their younger sibling with name-calling and horrible stories, telling them *they* are adopted. I was the big sister that told my little sister that *I* was adopted and that one day my real family would come for me. I was the odd one out, I was the one that did not belong. She could stay and be safe, but I had to go.

I would stare into the mirror, haunted by my reflection, looking for signs that I was not my father's daughter, looking for signs that I was someone else so that the shame could be bearable. If I was not really his daughter and I did not belong to this family, that would explain things. It would explain the abuse, because I was not actually his daughter, which meant he did not really break any unimaginable rules when he abused me, because I was not biologically his, so I was just like a stranger. He did not have to protect me or see me in another way because I was not his real daughter. If I was adopted, they did not need to love me the way they loved or protected my siblings. They did not need to value me because I was not actually one of them. I could be just another human sacrifice.

The mirror still haunts me today, when I catch glimpses of myself, my father's daughter. It is not just the mirror that can cause the pain of this reality. Mannerisms, movements, tone, even beliefs I have inherited from my father catch me off guard sometimes. They can disgust me and cause me to hate myself, the body that I live in, the body that is a part of him. Though I hold the beauty of my mother in many of my features, he shows himself, even in some of the photographs of me today, I see him looking back at me. I am my father's daughter and I see him in me. When I see him staring back at me, a part of me, staring down at me from the box seats of the arena I am reminded of how small I am, how easy it was for him to sacrifice me for the sake of himself. I am reminded that he believes me and my wellbeing to be less important than his, I am cruelly reminded of how dispensable I must be to him.

All of these alternative truths, the black sheep, the adopted daughter and many more I have spoken of throughout the years are all dreams of another truth to make the significance of facing the reality less ugly. They are the coping mechanisms I have used to remain in the arena, institutionalised to believe that there could be some form of safety in this common space.

Today, to break down the walls of the institution, as I dismantle the unsafe space and I attempt to deactivate the minefields on the mainland, I choose to no longer sacrifice myself. My parents no longer hold the power, and they can no longer expect my silent sacrifice. I am free from the torture of having my still-beating heart placed on the ground beside my body, free from the demands of the distant gods.

Today the sun still rises and the world around me remains. Life is valued, survivors no longer have to be victims and no one has to die for us to exist.

Ten

CAROLINE THE COMMODITY

My body carries many truths. It is a marvellous, ever-evolving entity that has the capacity to morph in ways I still do not fully understand. Yes, my body has the power to do incredible things. Some that I take for granted like the breaths that I take every day to keep myself alive. Then there are the more momentous occasions where my body has actually grown another human inside of it, every day over nine months, giving my babies exactly what they needed for life. In my body, I carry shame and love, but I also carry power. The elements of shame and power are often in conflict as I walk throughout the world in the body that you see.

I became aware of my body at a very young age, and I have shared the hunger that I craved when I realised my body had the capacity to draw attention to itself. When I discovered that I could have boys, men and even girls and women shower me with compliments about my body and my face and the value they held in the world. That kind of power, the power of being attractive and being valued for the way that I looked had some significant effects on my sense of self and self-worth from a very early age. Being aware of my body and the way that it was perceived by the world around me at the same time that the abuse commenced was a collision of emotions, forming a conflict within me, the tug of war between shame and power that I sometimes still experience to this day.

I was told as a teenager how attractive I was, and during this time I pursued ways to use this attraction from others to my benefit. Yes, that meant boyfriends and being a part of certain social groups in high school, but it also meant the start of my modelling career. The commodity of my body had already become clear to me. I could use my body to make money, people wanted to look at me and that gave me power. As a woman of colour, the way I looked was unusual in mainstream advertising and media. I was consistently praised for how exotic I looked and told how rare my look was in the industry. It was a special feeling knowing that the world found me attractive and that I had reached a value that had currency, beyond words and looks from admiring teenage boys.

The tug of war continued internally and I would fight with my body, feeling like it was a weapon I had little control over. Why was I continuing to embrace the attraction that I kept being told about, when it was causing me so much harm? Why did I believe that being attractive was a good thing, when it may have been the reason my father could not restrain himself from abusing me? Was the way that I looked too much to draw the line? Was my sexual appeal greater than the clear boundaries in place between a father and a daughter? Was it my fault the abuse occurred, my body's fault?

Writing these words makes me feel ill, as my body reminds me of how sick these thoughts are and my stomach churns. How horrible it is that I even have to come to terms with this reality. It is abhorrent that I cannot simply be proud of my beauty and love it for what it is. It is unjust that my beauty and sexuality have to carry this ugly truth, that it has been used as a weapon with the potential to destroy me. My mental health struggles with the tug of war of hating and loving my body, its beauty and the pain that it carries.

It is a tricky game, being valued for what you look like on the outside. Beauty is fleeting; it comes with youth and society tells us that as women our looks will fade and that we will not be worthy or valued once we age. We are told that only certain aesthetics are beautiful, but that we must compete with each other as women for the title of beautiful, that we must crave the spotlight and the gaze of men, keeping ourselves groomed and pretty to appeal to their visual desires. Creating a sense of value and self-worth based on the way that I looked was a dangerous beginning, and would continue to be something I struggled with for the majority of my young adult life.

I screamed internally, and even out loud sometimes about how angry it made me that I was only seen and valued for my body. I have had men only speak to me because they have hoped to have sex with me, frustrated when I persisted in keeping to the subject in conversations, whilst avoiding their sexual advances. I have had men tell me that they have only met with me in business settings in the hopes that they could change the conversation and make it sexual in some way. I have been told by business peers that they believe that I have only won business deals or had success because of the way that I look. I have had women pull their husbands away from me in social settings. I've even had women tell men not to befriend me whilst telling me to my face that I only get what I want because of the way that I look, because men only see me as worthwhile because of my body.

These women who are meant to be my allies turn their backs on me because of the weapon my body can be and the destruction they know it can cause. In many ways I understand that this is also likely to be the result of their own internalised misogyny from generations of living in a patriarchal society. Men have encouraged us as women to compete against each other for their praise and admiration. Men have consistently told us that there can only be one, the one that is the prettiest, the one that is the most desired woman in the room.

These are the same women that may read these words of mine and think, poor Caroline, a pretty girl who gets what she wants because of the way that she looks, why should I not turn away from her? Why should I feel sympathy and see her as a victim?

I will not lie; I have taken advantage of my sexual appeal many times in my lifetime. I have been overly forward and aggressive in seeking sexual partners. I have been the reason relationships have fractured or ended. I am not proud of my actions, nor do I use the abuse I have experienced to excuse my behaviour. In the past I have believed that I could use my body to be the predator, because if I took on that role that I would never be a victim again. Predator or prey? There was only one obvious choice. I had unwillingly been the prey as a child, I would therefore choose to be the opposite as an adult. I took control, pushing boundaries before they could be pushed on me. It was the safest way to be in control, the safest way my body would not be used against me.

I have used my looks to enter boardrooms, knowing that men were only inviting me to take a seat at the table for their own reasons, but pushing ahead nonetheless to succeed in business, rejecting their advances and proving that my intellect and capability was beyond their desires to only see me for my body.

At the same time of acting as my outwardly sexualised self I have mentioned how much I dreamt of flying under the radar. The secrets and the shame I have carried have been heavy and have caused me to wish that I could simply disappear. They have haunted me and it has angered me that I cannot simply be valued for everything else that I have to offer, all those things other than my looks. I have been desperate to be known for more than what I look like, desperate to prove my worth. Desperate to be more than one thing.

I have sought refuge from the male gaze, often walking straight past men I know who were trying to get my attention, blinkers on, trying not to make eye contact because of the fear and exhaustion of only being seen as a body. Fear of the sickening feeling that can come when my body is at risk, knowing what some predatory men think when they look at my body. There is an anger that lives in me in those times, those times when I have been brave, or maybe reckless when spending time with men who have intentions different to mine. I nevertheless always remembered what my body has survived so far, and have thought, *what could be worse than surviving my father's abuse?* These men could not do any damage worse than what he did.

In this moment of what seems to be defiance, I choose my own body, I know its power, I am proud of its beauty and I am aware of the innocence it had taken away from it. It has a fearlessness that can only come by rising above the tragedy that is childhood sexual abuse.

Today I am whole in myself. Yes, I am still successfully building a modelling career. I do this in a way that respects my body and its beauty. I am the face of my businesses and continue to explore ways to stretch myself and show up every day, bringing value to the projects and ventures I am passionate about. I am now comfortable in being a commodity, knowing that my currency is more than my body, it is my lived experience, my kindness and my integrity. I am in control and my choices are ones that I own, because they belong to me.

I have chosen to honour my body and to no longer be at war with it. There are many women in the world who have survived the kind of abuse I have. These survivors have gone on to change their bodies significantly. From how they carry themselves, shrinking themselves to become invisible or puffing themselves up to seem stronger. Some have morphed and gained weight in hopes of no longer being attractive enough to be abused again, to escape notice, to be overlooked, to be safe. Some have numbed their pain with drugs and alcohol, the effects of these substances ravishing their bodies. By ending the war with my body, I can confidently say that my body no longer belongs to my abuser or anyone else and its value is not quantified by their opinions or looks of admiration or desire. It is not used as a weapon, nor seen as one. As a person, I have a power far greater than the aesthetic beauty of my physical body, and have a value that will hold its worth, many years after I no longer live on this earth.

Eleven

DISCOVERY IN CAMBODIA

One of the wonderful things about being an entrepreneur and being my own boss is the opportunities I can give to myself and the people I meet along the way. I had a café that I frequented, where the owner and I would chat about business and family and over time we formed a really great friendship. In 2017 he emailed me, copying in another friend of his, introducing the two of us. With the simple words, 'I think you are both awesome women, and I think you will get along really well,' he handed this opportunity of connection over to us, leaving the next steps in our hands. I trusted in his observation, as he is a great guy and I knew that he would not have made such an effort to connect us if he did not feel that we would get along. I contacted the woman in the email, organising a coffee catch up at the café that our mutual friend owned.

I don't often have coffee with people I have never met before unless it is for a more formal business meeting or to meet a new client. The whole thing felt a bit like a blind date, which was incredibly awkward but as soon as we began to chat, I could see exactly why our friend had wanted to introduce us. We were both businesswomen, both incredibly driven and both looking for ways to make a positive impact in the world.

A friendship was formed over coffee that day and I am forever grateful to our mutual friend who introduced us. Over the next year, I watched my new friend continue to stretch herself and take on wonderful opportunities, one of which was a trip to Cambodia to participate in the Project Gen Z Dare to Dream program. The program involved a group of business owners and entrepreneurs running workshops at Sunrise Cambodia, an organisation that supports and provides a home for displaced orphans and disadvantaged children.

I saw a lot of my new friend before she left for Cambodia and was struck by how hard she had been working to meet the fundraising goals and targets mandated by the project. The real eye-opening moment was seeing her after she returned from Cambodia - in what almost seemed like a physical change, she was transformed. I could see how much the trip had opened her eyes to the vast differences between Australia and Cambodia and how the experience had changed her forever. As my new friend worked with teenagers here in Australia her main observations were around the mental health of the Cambodian children and how resilient they were compared to Australian children who were more prone to ill mental health.

My interest was sparked and I started investigating how I could participate in this incredible program. I first had to conquer my inner critic, the voice in my head that was telling me that I was not enough of an entrepreneur to attend. I was not sure if I had enough experience in business or the skills the program would be looking for. After a call with the founder of Project Gen Z, it was clear that I was eligible, so she sent me through the application details and held a place for me on the upcoming 2018 trip. Then came the next hurdle. I not only had to source the funds to attend the trip, to cover my flights and accommodation, but I also had to fundraise. Fundraising a specific amount was a non-negotiable requirement for attending the trip and I was not sure how I would fit that in whilst also running my new business and caring for my young family.

My husband is also a business owner and our household is a busy one, to say the least, so when we looked at the trip's specified dates it was also clear that the timing was going to be a significant challenge. My husband would be working on a major interstate event during the trip. With little local support to care for our children, it would take too much juggling for me to be overseas for two weeks whilst he managed his major event and also looked after our children.

Reluctantly I parked the idea. I called the founder of Project Gen Z and declined my spot for the trip. It was early 2018 and I had other things I needed to focus on. My new friend had committed to the 2018 trip; her experience had been so life-changing that she was itching to get back to Cambodia and work with the children again. Though I was very disappointed that I would not be joining her, there were various upcoming fundraising events in the calendar as the Project Gen Z team prepared to travel to Cambodia again, so there were many other ways that I could support them in their efforts, namely helping them fundraise.

After coming to terms with the fact that I was not attending the trip that year, my husband and I attended a fundraising dinner. It was fascinating to see the room full of Project Gen Z alumni and the camaraderie they shared. Some of the people in the room had not been together in person since their trip in the previous October and their love for each other as they reunited, the bond that they shared and their excitement to be together as they fundraised for the upcoming trip was indisputable.

During the evening an auction was scheduled and many items were displayed, including some that I had donated myself, for the guests to bid on. Some were silent auction items, where we simply placed our name and our bid on a piece of paper, waiting for the results at the end of the evening. The major items were auctioned in a lively way, the auctioneer being a seasoned real estate professional and also a Project Gen Z alumnus. The room was buzzing as he joked with guests, enticing them to bid on items, encouraging them to outbid their neighbours at nearby tables, all in the name of fundraising for Sunrise. The room was electric, the noise of our chatter rising as we all became more and more competitive and added to the chaos of the auction.

The live auction occurred towards the end of the evening, very strategically to say the least as my husband had already had a few glasses of red wine by this stage. I personally do not like to get involved in bidding; in many ways in life, I am competitive, mainly competing with myself and setting ridiculous goals and benchmarks to reach. I often become an introvert, however, when it comes to public displays of competitiveness. I can be strategic though, whispering to the person next to me, encouraging them to bid for things on my behalf so that I do not need to be the person yelling out and adding to the hype. With this in mind, and with my husband fuelled by the flowing red wine it should have been obvious to me what was going to happen next.

The last item was being announced. A place in the 2018 Cambodia trip, at a set price for the travel costs, but without the usual additional requirement to fundraise the full fundraising amount. My husband looked over at me, quietly asking me, 'Do you want to bid?' I laughed! We had been over this discussion, the dates were not suitable, we had a million other things that we had to juggle, but here he was open to bidding for my place on the trip. He put his hand up, calling out his first bid and the room erupted. The banter went back and forth between my husband and another bidder at a table towards the front of the room. It was entertaining, to say the least, the room getting louder at each round of bids. In what felt like seconds the auctioneer called out, 'Going once, going twice, SOLD! to the gentleman at the back!' and that was it, I was going to Cambodia!

We would spend the next day trying - as my poor husband nursed his sore head - to work out how exactly we were going to juggle me being away for two weeks. Calls were made to my mother-in-law, who agreed to come to stay with my husband and our children to provide him with some support so he could also travel for his own work commitments during this time. I began to fundraise, organise, and make plans to be away and before I knew it, I was at the airport, surrounded by fellow entrepreneurs, on my way to Cambodia.

I had not been on a trip like this with a big group of people since my days of school camps in high school. I had only travelled overseas with loved ones and family members so to be on my own with a group of strangers, other than my new friend who had attended the trip the year prior, was liberating. I had the freedom to only focus on myself and immerse myself in the experience. As a mother, there isn't anything quite like travelling without your children and being able to put yourself first.

During our flight to Cambodia, I had the opportunity to chat with lots of new people, people who I now class as some of my closest friends, and they shared with me how much the previous trips had changed their lives. They gently guided me on what I might experience, the challenges and emotions I would face and how fast-paced the trip would be.

The trip consisted of two parts. In the first half, we would spend time together in a personal and professional development setting. We would travel to historic locations in Cambodia, exploring the culture and history of the country. We would take this time to form a bond as a group, talking about business and life whilst also reflecting on the places we were visiting. A key part of this first half of the trip focused on the history of Cambodia, and most importantly the role of the Khmer Rouge, also known as the Communist Party of Kampuchea.

The Khmer Rouge was a brutal regime that ruled Cambodia from 1975 to 1979, under the leadership of notorious dictator Pol Pot. In Pot's attempt to create a Cambodian 'master race' through social engineering his regime was responsible for the deaths of more than two million people in Cambodia. Those killed were either executed as enemies of the regime or died from starvation, disease or damage to their bodies sustained during back-breaking work or abuse. Those seen as intellectuals or potential leaders of a revolutionary movement were also executed. Survivors have stated that some people were executed for merely appearing to be intellectuals, for such things as wearing glasses or being able to speak a foreign language.

The Vietnamese Army invaded Cambodia in 1979 and removed Pol Pot and the Khmer Rouge from power after a series of violent battles on the border between the two countries. Over the decades since the fall of the Khmer Rouge, Cambodia has gradually re-established ties with the world. The country still faces significant problems including widespread poverty and illiteracy.

Almost 40 years later, the challenges of the Cambodian people were glaringly obvious to me as I left the comforts of my suburban middle-class life in Australia, to be confronted first-hand with the Cambodian people's reality. The trauma and impacts of the Khmer Rouge were still clearly visible, not only in the physical state of certain parts of the country itself but also in the sheer numbers of orphans and displaced children, unable to find the comfort of a safe home due to the atrocities that had occurred to their parents and grandparents.

When speaking with my fellow Project Gen Z members prior to visiting Sunrise and commencing our workshops with the children, one of them had spoken of the importance of not showing emotional overwhelm or sadness in front of the children. We were encouraged not to cry or show negative emotions if possible. This was because some of the children did not speak English and due to the language barriers, they would often assume the tears were a sign that they had done something wrong. We were encouraged to seek support from our fellow Project Gen Z members when overwhelmed and to unpack our thoughts and emotions at the end of the day, away from the children.

In addition to clear child safety rules such as not being alone with children and not entering the dorm rooms where the children slept, we were also asked not to ask the children questions about why they were living at Sunrise, what had happened to them or anything about their past. If we sought details about a specific child, we were to speak with the Sunrise staff who would provide us with information if they felt it was suitable. Speaking about their lives could be triggering for the children and we were invited into the community to coach as entrepreneurs, not to be counsellors to the children or expecting them to relive their trauma.

I remember my first day at Sunrise like it was yesterday. We arrived in our convoy of tuk-tuk vehicles, we were already hot and sweaty simply from the heat of the day, our skin sticky from the dirt and dust that was kicked up from the roads that we had travelled on.

We waited outside of the gate so we could enter the centre as one group, although we could already hear the children behind the concrete walls. There were giggles and shrieks of excitement, with many of the children eager to be reunited with some of the members of Project Gen Z who they had met in previous years. It was exciting and nerve-wracking all at once. I knew I was in safe hands, travelling with my friend who had attended the trip before but I very much felt out of my comfort zone. The nervousness created butterflies in my stomach and my skin prickled with sweat, both from the relentless heat and humidity but also from the anticipation building in my stomach.

My thoughts bounced back and forth, thinking about my own children and how I would never wish for them to be without myself or my husband, orphaned and abandoned. My thoughts then rushed to my place as a survivor of abuse, knowing there would likely be children at Sunrise who had experienced abuse similar to mine. Somehow, I had not given this part of my story any real consideration when signing up for the trip but at this moment I was struck by this thought. No one on the trip, not even my friend, knew that I was a survivor of childhood sexual abuse, and due to the intensity and excitement of the moment I quickly had to put this thought aside and immerse myself in the moment. I had not even acknowledged the connection of the stories up until this point, not considering that my story could be similar to the stories of these children. Being a mother myself and a survivor of abuse, I felt vulnerable and on alert all at once, and I hadn't even come face to face with any of the children yet. All of these thoughts tumbled through my mind in the minutes before I stepped into the gates of Sunrise.

Entering the space, I was met with an experience that stirred my senses. It was so colourful, the walls of the buildings splashed with bright colours, similar to what I would see at a school or early childhood centre in Australia, yet there were some clear differences to the schools I had worked with there. Many of the children were in second-hand clothes, some did not wear shoes and had some visible signs of abuse, such as scars on their faces and bodies, the physical evidence of the life they had lived prior to seeking refuge and safety at Sunrise.

The sound was exhilarating and it became even louder as we entered further into the gates of Sunrise. The children started to scream and shout with excitement, they surrounded us and I was pulled in different directions by children who were eager to meet me or to show me around. Some of the children surrounded us in outer circles, nervously not wanting to get too close, especially to the new Project Gen Z members like myself who were strangers to them.

We were ushered into the main hall of the centre where we were seated, ready to be welcomed by the Sunrise staff and the children. The founder of Project Gen Z thanked the Sunrise community on our behalf for welcoming us with open arms and also took the opportunity to talk about the work we were planning to do over the coming days and the schedule that was outlined for us. There were further eruptions of noise as the Project Gen Z founder hyped up the students, fuelling their inquisitive minds and spurring on their competitive nature.

In many ways this was no different to being in a school hall back in Australia, watching kids stomp their feet and carry on, trying to see who could be the loudest and gain the most attention from the visitors to their school.

As we sat to watch performances by the children, I started to observe a few things, some of the first signs of vulnerability that I would go on to notice more and more over the coming days. A young girl, 13 or 14 years old with big brown eyes and long black hair would give me a sheepish smile every time I looked in her direction. She had already taken a liking to me. She eagerly sat next to me in the hall and had even pushed other children away, trying hard to be as close to me as possible. However, every time I would show her any attention, even just a smile in her direction I would see her retreat, shrink into herself and try to deflect the attention, urging me to look back at the stage.

This went on for the entire performance; the less attention I gave her, the more she would become comfortable, at one stage she pressed her knee against mine as a sign of comfort. Though in each moment I would look at her or try to speak to her she would retreat, made nervous by my attention.

That afternoon the children were split into groups and given their team colours. The Project Gen Z group were also split up and told which teams of children we would be coaching for the upcoming Dare to Dream challenge. By chance, the young girl who had sat next to me during the welcome performance was in my team and over the coming days, I would see her retreat less and less, forming a bond with me over a very short period of time.

This girl was one of many that took my breath away, and there were many times I had to excuse myself from the group space to compose myself and manage my overwhelming emotions. I would catch myself, eyes welling up with tears, a lump in my throat, knowing I had to compose myself because I knew that if the tears began to flow, I might not be able to stop them. I would look upwards, attempting to will the tears back inside myself. Pressing my tongue to the roof of my mouth, I would stand, breathing deep breaths to slow the tears from coming.

I was struck by how incredible these children were. They showed outstanding levels of intelligence and adaptability, but most of all they had visible traits of resilience. No challenge we set them was too great. When we pushed them out of their comfort zones they simply worked harder. Failure was not an option. They wanted to take every second with us and make magic with those seconds, knowing the value of the entrepreneurial lessons we were sharing with them.

There were moments where I would forget where I was, moments where it felt that I was just at a school in Australia, hosting an educational workshop. Then I would look around and see the faces of these children, knowing that many of them were orphaned and likely survivors of abuse. Some of the effects of the abuse were hard to hide, evidence that I could not unsee. There were children who had scars, some who clearly showed the visible effects of neglect and malnutrition prior to their time at Sunrise. Some of the children had scarring across their faces where they had been punished with acid, sometimes purposely made to look more vulnerable to increase their capacity to beg for money when on the streets, where they were then expected to hand that money over to their abusers who kept them captive.

There was no looking away, no hiding the fact that these children had already been through so much, but at this moment, they were taking this opportunity to learn from us. This was their opportunity to thrive. They knew how to survive; they had done so prior to Sunrise and had already experienced the shift from victim to survivor. In doing so they filled us with admiration and love, taking every moment they could to soak up the lessons we were passing on to them as a way to make a difference to their futures.

In the last days of my time at Sunrise, I was speaking with an older girl, no longer living at Sunrise but who had been invited back to participate in workshops. She talked openly to me about her siblings and her family situation, explaining how she had come to live in the Sunrise community. I was mindful not to ask her too many questions; we had been given strict instructions not to question the children and to respect their privacy. This girl went on to share more with me about her parents and guardians, the neglect she had experienced and how grateful she was to Sunrise and the impact the community had made in her life.

When speaking about her family I was struck by the tenderness she had in her words towards them. There was no anger or resentment, there was almost a sense of relief in her tone. At that moment I chose to ask a question; I asked her if she would return back to her family if she could, even knowing what her life was like at Sunrise in comparison to her life with her family. She simply replied, 'Yes, I would go home, they are my family and I belong with them.'

I was baffled, though I carefully did not express my confusion to her; it was not my place to tell her all of the reasons why I thought she was wrong. Even though

I knew that returning to her family was not really an option for her I sat there in slight disbelief that she would still choose to go back, especially after knowing how much better life was away from them.

Time moved quickly during the days at Sunrise and conversations like this one were fleeting. We were in the middle of a team challenge so even within the depths of this conversation that would go on to change my views on family and belonging, I moved on from the conversation and dived into the organised chaos of the remainder of our days. On our last night with the Sunrise children, we celebrated the teams, all that we had achieved together and announced how much money had been raised for Sunrise through the prior fundraising and the efforts of the children during the challenge. It was a wonderful evening which ended in tears and deeply moving goodbyes.

I cried a lot on that last night. My heart had expanded rapidly over those few days with the Sunrise children. I was amazed at how quickly I had formed a bond with some of the children and I did not want to leave. Though I missed my own children terribly and knew that I needed to head home, a part of me wanted to take the Sunrise children home with me, knowing how many opportunities and privileges I could offer them back in Australia.

I had seen the glaring similarities between myself and the children and it was confronting to face the fact that children who grew up in a war-torn country felt a similar pain and longing to children just like me. In the end, our core needs outweighed logic in our decisions. Belonging was chosen over safety. The pain in this realisation was raw and the common need in these children and in myself to survive sat at our core. There was also a new understanding of the helplessness and vulnerability of our childhoods and how in many ways we simply do not have a choice in where we are and what happens to us.

The Project Gen Z team had planned our trip well; members of the team who had participated in previous trips were acutely aware of the impact the time at Sunrise had on each individual and how much time to decompress was needed after our time at Sunrise, before travelling home, back to Australia.

We spent our remaining days in Cambodia together, enjoying the luxury of being tucked away in our hotel, embracing the benefits our privilege could buy us as we drank cocktails by the pool. Though it was nice to relax, it did feel strange being in such a lavish environment. It was jarring and I felt guilty in a way after running around with over a hundred Cambodian children in the days prior. I knew I was still shaken internally after seeing myself in the children. Something had shifted in me, and it made me uneasy knowing how similar I was to these children. That in many ways, the amount of privilege I had experienced in my life did not remove the fact that I was a survivor of childhood abuse and that I too had chosen family and belonging over an alternative life I knew could exist for me.

On one of our last evenings in Cambodia, our Project Gen Z group sat together, unpacking our personal experiences from the days together and connecting on a deeper level. The tone was set really quickly as we went around the group, with each person talking quite vulnerably about how the trip had affected them, what they had learnt about themselves and what they felt they would be taking home with them.

At this moment, in this safe space with my new Project Gen Z family, I chose to tell them about the abuse. I shared how I had experienced childhood sexual abuse at the hands of my father, that my mother had not left when I disclosed to her and how I had and continued to remain in our family setting, keeping this secret from my sister. I shared the heaviness of this, the heartbreak of it all and what I had seen in the children of Sunrise. How I had seen myself in them - I had seen first-hand what children look like when they are abused. I had seen the gratitude and hope in their eyes and in the same moment the desperation to belong, the invisible strings that connected them to their families, even when they knew they were not safe in their care.

There was not one dry eye amongst the group that night. We had already shed tears for each other as each and every one of us shared the depths of their experience and how the trip had changed them. Not only was this moment significant for me in realising how much I was still tied to my family, but it was also the first moment I had really used my voice to share my truth. With a group of people, who weeks prior were strangers to me, I was held safely by them and given the opportunity to feel a little lighter as I unpacked the complexities around wanting to belong, despite the detriment to myself and my values.

I had met other survivors before my trip to Cambodia. I had attended events where keynote speakers had talked about their abuse and how they had survived. I had read books and articles sharing detailed accounts of the harm-doers that lived in the world. I knew I wasn't alone in the community of survivors. The stats were there for anybody to see. The children of Sunrise helped me see myself in their stories. They mirrored 10-year-old Caroline and spoke for her, speaking for her desire to belong and to be a part of a safe and loving family.

I will forever be grateful to the children of Sunrise for showing me there is another way. That I no longer need to neglect myself in order to love myself. That I can thrive, creating a new family and a new place to call home.

Twelve

THE DEPTHS OF ANGER

"The truth will set you free, but first, it will piss you off."
– Gloria Steinem

Pissed off is an understatement when it comes to how I have felt at times. The first word that comes to mind is angry, however even angry may not really cut it. Enraged, furious and outraged may come a little closer depending on the day, though today I will stick with angry. I have been angry at specific people in my family, angry at the people who should have done more, and at times, I have extended the anger out to the entire world. I have felt failed by the world we live in, by what trauma has done to the generations before me and what that has meant for my lived experience.

When we label our emotions and simplify them with just one word, we often forget about the depths of the emotion and what likely lives under the surface of that emotion.

Deep inside the anger lives disappointment; I have continued to be disappointed by both of my parents for various reasons. There are disappointments that live in my father's actions when he began to abuse me, the disappointment that his love for me and the need to protect me as my father was not greater than his sexual desires. There is a disappointment that my mother did not see the signs of the abuse when it was occurring, that she missed the signs that I was changing and withdrawing more and more each day. There is also disappointment in her actions, or lack thereof, when I disclosed to her and she did not leave him or choose to take myself and my sister away. I am disappointed that I was expected to remain in our family setting, expected to play a false role that would deteriorate my wellbeing for years. Somewhere in all of that, I am also disappointed in myself. I am disappointed that I did not have the courage to speak up sooner, that I did not leave our family and that I chose, if it was ever really a choice, to remain in our family setting, keeping the truth from my sister for over 27 years.

In addition to the disappointment, deep inside the anger, there lives a deep shame. Shame that my body has been abused in this way, tainted by a touch I never wanted or deserved. Shame that this touch came from the hands of my own father. There is a shame that I was not worthy or loved enough and that I was seen as something that could be taken, that I was not enough to protect, I was just another victim. The shame that I had collapsed inside of myself, frozen with no words. The shame that I carry when remembering that I could not find my voice for four years, the voice that could have stopped the abuse from happening over and over again. I carry a deep shame that my mother has chosen my father over me, reminding me again that my value is questioned, that I am not as worthy as I wish I could be, that I am somehow *less than*.

In the anger, next to the disappointment and the shame, I carry sadness. My heart is broken. A love that is meant to be endless and unbreakable is severed. I sit in the sadness of my truth and yearn for a different reality. I am sad that I do not have the parents I deserve. Sad that I did not get to experience my childhood with the freedom of safety, enjoying my innocence and that I was not allowed to make safe, happy memories. I am sad about the choices I made as a teenager. Knowing how much potential I had but how much the trauma derailed my adolescence, causing me to numb when I should have been enjoying some of the most formative years of my life. I feel the deep sadness in the decisions I have made today, the decision to live on my island away from the mainland, knowing that it now serves me to preserve myself and my values, but in turn that the decision means that there is heartbreak at the loss and grief of estranging myself from my parents. Disconnecting them from the child I was, the woman I am and the woman I am becoming.

Rising up from the anger next to the disappointment, shame and sadness, there is a white-hot rage that surges up. A rage in knowing I am not special, not only not special enough to not be spared of the sexual abuse, but also, not special in that my story in many ways is not unique. The rage that I am filled with when I hear of children who are experiencing the same abuse that I encountered, the rage when I read that 20% of girls in Australia have been sexually abused and that 90 to 95% of this abuse has been committed by men. At this very moment as I write these words there is a child being sexually abused by an adult. As you read my words, are you not also filled with rage?

Is your rage also terror as you consider how little control you may have when this abuse occurs? When you realise how commonplace childhood sexual abuse is? The rage for me bubbles over and I often lash out in ridiculous, meaningless moments, knowing that the fuel of the rage is something deeper than that particular moment. Knowing that the rage is a desperate craving to understand why adults sexually abuse children and how we can stop it from happening. The rage is the scariest part of the anger, the depths of the anger that I choose to control the most. I have learnt that not much can be achieved when you are rage-fuelled and yelling at someone. But I know it is there, sitting under the surface, the rage under the anger.

In the past, the anger has caused me to do some significant damage to the people around me and the relationships that we have. The anger has been a result of fear, often being triggered by my vulnerability. In times when I have felt the comfort of joy and peace in a relationship with a loved one, a small voice has whispered inside of me, reminding me not to trust the safety of the joy. The trust between myself and my parents was broken at such an early age and this pattern of having difficulty in trusting others has continued throughout my entire life. I have even found myself being frightened of the love and vulnerability that comes with loving my own children at times, waiting for the day they hurt me and cause me pain similar to the pain that my parents have inflicted. If my parents have the capacity to cause such pain, what would make my children any different? Can you imagine the anger that creates in me, when I realise I am too scared to fully love my children, due to my own experiences as a child?

This pattern of using anger to cause damage has long been a way to deflect and protect. I have chosen at times to start arguments or act irrationally to remind myself that when things feel too good to be true that they likely are too good to be true. As I write these words, I feel sad for myself, sad that I have been conditioned to question love and never believing that it could really be unconditional. This anger, layered with sadness and all of the other emotions I have described is heavy, an exhausting existence I have lived for far too many years.

This system of needing to have the upper hand was a pattern I lived in for many years. Causing conflict and damaging aspects of my relationships so I could then go in and fix them provided me with a sense of control. I would then fall into a sense of comfortability and safety, though those moments would be fleeting as the voice in my head would whisper, 'It's too good to be true...' Off I would go to create chaos, to prove that it could not really ever be as good as I had hoped. I would cause damage, fix the problem, find comfort, be sceptical, feel the fear, react in the moment and cause more damage. It all sounds exhausting, doesn't it?

This pattern continued for years, without me really knowing the long-term damage I was doing to myself and the people I loved. In being failed by my parents and using my relationship with them as a model I had convinced myself that there was only one way to love, that it was risky and that it likely would not last. I believed that the only way I and the people around me could love each other was also by hurting each other.

There are people in my life to whom I owe a deep apology. People who have been on the receiving end of my bursts of anger and fear. Some of them have withstood these repeated outbursts and my attempt to push them away and I'm grateful to them for persevering, I am grateful that they have chosen to keep loving me despite my numerous attempts to tell them I was not worth their love.

I have found a sense of peace in my vulnerability. The peace comes from experiencing deep human connections and love. I have experienced this depth when I have embraced my vulnerability. It helps that I now surround myself with people that I deeply trust. However, that peace in my vulnerability also comes in knowing that my anger is valid. That my emotions and each layer of the anger are a part of my truth. In my truth I can be more than one thing. I can be at peace in my integrity and I can also be pissed off.

Thirteen

HEARTBREAKS, GOODBYES AND GRIEF

There was a moment recently that I was speaking with a trusted friend, and I described to her the state that I was in emotionally. I felt I had crept into a dark hole and couldn't find my way out. This feeling of loneliness and abandonment was all-consuming, often creeping in when I least expected it. Although I had confidently made the decision to estrange myself from my father, and in more recent times to also estrange myself from my mother, I still found myself in a depth of darkness that I could not escape. This darkness was a place lurking in between the mainland and my island, it was a place devoid of hope, a place that filled me with confusion and self-doubt as I tried to find the confidence in my decisions.

I have been classed by a previous psychology professional as a high functioning trauma survivor. I am incredibly determined. I am articulate and confident in my truth; I can speak openly about the trauma and I have a way of simply getting on with life, even when I am struggling in traumatic environments or working through the impacts that they have had on me. Nevertheless, over these particular few months in the darkness, I caught myself weeping unexpectedly. Sometimes I would justify these outbursts as a result of the sad movie I was watching or an upsetting news article I had read online, but there were also times where the tears would simply fall, falling at times in moments that seemed out of place. I knew that something was really deeply wrong when I was playing with my border collie puppy and found myself cuddling him while tears streamed from my eyes. He stared up at me with his curious little face, likely wondering what was happening to his human who was suddenly sobbing and making noises that were not common at all. In this state of my full-blown ugly cry, I was lost. Why was a decision I was actively making, a decision to look after myself and put myself first causing me so much pain? Why was this transition so difficult for me?

When I shared with a friend about this moment, about how I had been inconsolably crying, how I had felt that I was in the depths of this confusing pain, she listened to me, and simply said, 'You're experiencing grief.' With her words, at this moment it was like a light bulb was suddenly switched on in the dark hole I was in, and though I was still inside the hole I could look around me, not as frightened by the darkness, because of having a word to explain the feelings I felt and the experience that I was living.

In the months prior to this discussion, I had been doing some incredibly challenging personal work. Work I was not even aware of, the kind of deep emotional work I did not have words to describe. I was experiencing the heartbreak of leaving the mainland for good. I had made it clear to my family members that I was no longer choosing to live there. In speaking my truth, I was moving away, making a home for myself on my island. What I did not realise was that in making that choice I was breaking up with a life that I had always known. I was ending something and moving away from a place that I had always called home. The actor had spoken her last line. The scene had ended and there I was, *Caroline the person,* standing in the darkness trying to work out who I was when I was not acting and what would come next.

I knew that I had to leave to survive, that in speaking my truth I could no longer also remain in the place where my truth was silenced. Though sometimes even when we know that we are doing the right thing, knowing does not make the doing any less hard.

I love my mother; I have reached for her many times and asked her to come with me. I have asked her to do better and to walk beside me. But she has chosen not to. In moments when she has expressed how much it breaks her heart to lose me, she has simultaneously chosen to remain on the mainland. In moments she has told me how much she misses me, she has also stayed in a relationship with my father, knowing that not only is he an abuser, but that he abused *me*.

Making the choice to say goodbye to her has been one of the hardest decisions I have ever made. I had remained tethered to her and our mother-daughter bond as a way of holding on to something I had always wished I had in its entirety. I had distracted myself, ignoring the choices she had made that had caused me significant trauma, to accept the life we had together. Choosing to only ever read from the script. Choosing to be a good daughter, a good girl. In stepping away I did not have the option to only keep the good; I could no longer only look away from the hurt she had caused, so I had to look away from it all, to leave the mainland completely and say goodbye.

In this goodbye, I underestimated the level of grief I would experience. Though grief is a natural response to loss, it can cause emotional suffering that at times can be unbearable. In my grief, I have experienced anger and disbelief. I have walked the peaks and valleys. Sometimes spending weeks in the valleys of my sadness, ugly crying and barely leaving my home. I have reached the peaks, sometimes forgetting that my grief exists, getting on with life, then feeling surprised at myself that I would dare ignore the reality of the pain, venturing back into the valley to experience moments of despair.

I often wonder if my current state of grief is similar to what I would experience if my mother had passed away. I know that it is unlikely that the feeling of grief is exactly the same, as she has not passed, I can pick up the phone and call her at any time, I can go back to the mainland if I wish to, I can pretend that everything is ok to regain the relationship we had. Sometimes in my mind, I have to pretend she has passed, so I do not feel the overwhelming guilt that I am being selfish. The guilt that sits heavy on my heart as I acknowledge that she is getting older, that time is passing and that she will indeed physically pass one day. Will I be angry at myself for not simply 'getting over it'? Will I regret the decisions I have made and the time we are losing when we are apart, separated by the vast ocean between the mainland and my island? Have I made the right decision? Only time will tell.

I believe that this is the part of my grief that haunts me the most, knowing that it did not need to be this way. Knowing that I am choosing to move away from the mainland, moving away from my mother, choosing to say goodbye. These moments of goodbye and the boundaries in place as I move from the mainland are clear in my mind. I feel the pain of them as the emotion rises from my stomach, rising up to my throat as it constricts, and the tighter it gets, the hotter my face feels. I continue to feel flushed as the tears begin to well in my eyes. I still have this sensation every time I remember the day I asked my mother not to call me on my birthday, declining her attempted call. The tears fall as I recall looking into her eyes a few months later as she told me how much she misses me, but that she would continue to respect my boundaries. Staring at her, watching her heart break before my eyes. Saying goodbye again that day, my last day on the mainland.

The grief is also in the knowledge that my mother is choosing not to take my hand when I reach for her, that she is instead choosing to remain on the mainland with my father. The heartbreak and grief feel the deepest when I am reminded by the choices that have been made by both of us, but sometimes the depth of my grief comes when I feel I have no choice at all.

Because if I do not choose myself, then who will?

Fourteen

RUMBLINGS ON UNEASY FOUNDATIONS

Momentum was building. *I* was building momentum. Since entering the space of being a business owner and entrepreneur I was finding my voice. More and more over the years, the voice I was cultivating was confident. I was often in rooms with high profile people, being given the opportunity to meet with them for business presentations and contract negotiations. I had to quickly find the bravery to speak up for myself and my business. This may seem like an expected part of the job of being a business owner or entrepreneur but when you are a woman of colour, in her early thirties, meeting with older men, often well established in their careers and positions, it can be incredibly daunting to present to them and convince them that your words have value.

What I did not realise was while I was actively building my reputation as a ruthless and determined businesswoman, I was also building my voice to speak openly about the things that were important to me. I was proudly wearing my badge as a feminist and actively searching for ways to support women around the world. I worked with organisations that were doing amazing work for women and girls. I spoke openly about the gender biases I had personally experienced and I donated to charities, seeking ways to support their work.

There was a running theme in the organisations I supported; they all had a focus on women and children, often supporting children who had been abused. These organisations were working to advocate for change in this space. To this day, they continue to work not only at a grassroots level but also in lobbying government departments and decision-makers to make significant, desperately needed changes in child safety.

As my career grew, I continued to speak up, volunteering and highlighting the organisations I was supporting. Working with these not-for-profit organisations was helping me find my voice, though at the same time I was aware of an uneasy shift under my footing. I've shared with you my experience of foundations and the uneasy and unreliable pieces I had attempted to build on when my parents were my first building blocks. Anyone who has lived in a place that experiences frequent earthquakes knows that the foundation they build on forms a vital part of the integrity of the building itself. Its longevity relies on the foundation's ability to withstand the rumblings that can turn into catastrophic waves, knocking the entire structure to the ground.

The rumblings I was experiencing were not exclusively external to me. There was an inner voice telling me that I was a fraud! Yes, I was taking small opportunities each and every day to speak my truth, to disclose the abuse to small groups of people and to speak publicly, with hidden language signalling to my fellow survivors that I was one of them. Yes, I was publicly supporting not-for-profit organisations, fundraising for them, volunteering with them and being an advocate for the great work they were doing. But my inner voice was screaming, every time I quietly spoke out, in every dollar I fundraised, there was a voice that would scream 'FRAUD!' A voice that told me that I could not be an advocate and continue to keep this secret from my sister, I could not be an advocate and continue to live on the mainland. In this instance, I could not continue to be more than one thing.

Everywhere I looked, things were changing around me. Voices were getting louder. In 2006 Tarana Burke started the Me Too movement, acknowledging her childhood sexual abuse and supporting survivors of both childhood and adult abuse by developing a vision to bring resources, support, and pathways of healing. The #metoo hashtag went viral in 2017 and, while its specific focus was highlighting sexual misconduct against adult survivors, I found myself saying those words publicly: Me Too.

Like most of the people who wrote the words #metoo on their social media, I was amazed and saddened at how many women spoke up over that time, at the sheer number of women in my life, some who were close to me, who had a story similar to mine. I was starting to believe that the fall of 'The Man' was coming, that perpetrators were being called out and that justice, long overdue, was on its way. The ground below me continued to shift, and I continued to feel uneasy speaking so openly in one way and hiding my truth in another.

Whilst trying to find some kind of solid ground I also knew that the turbulence and groundswell were from stories that were not mine to tell. There were other survivors of my father's wrongdoing. Some that had disclosed to me personally. Some that I knew were likely staying silent in a way to protect me and the mainland I lived on, similar to how I was choosing to create a world for my sister in which she could continue to see our father as one of the good guys. There were survivors out there who didn't know of the abuse I had experienced and believed that they were protecting my view of my father and my home on the mainland.

What began as a movement in Me Too became something I couldn't look away from. I found myself angrier each and every day as yet more men were called out for their behaviour. I watched our heroes fall, some that I never thought could be capable of such horrible things. I watched as beloved celebrities, politicians and other significant men in the public eye showed us all that they could be more than one thing. Monsters masquerading as men were unmasked. Every day another man was called out for abusing his power at the expense and sacrifice of young girls and women. Every day another man showed us that he could be more than one thing, just like my father.

The monumental efforts I was making to secure the earth under my feet was indescribable. To the detriment to myself and my mental health, I continued to watch these other men be called out, publicly named and shamed whilst I continued to keep my own father's secrets and protect my sister from the truth.

I cannot recall exactly what happened on the day I chose to knock down the arena myself. The day I decided to start again, smashing a wrecking ball into the entirety of my life so I could really be free from its chains. In that first blow, the moment I chose to say, 'No more,' I didn't know what was to come next or how long this journey would take.

Some days I feel as though I am still climbing out from under the rubble that caved in on me when I destroyed it all. The heaviest stones are the shame. Not only have I been weighed down by the shame of being a sexual abuse survivor, but it is also compounded by the horrific shame of the abuse being incestuous. Some days there is a heaviness that I carry when I know that the journey isn't over and may never be over. It is an ongoing lived experience. It is my life.

I have had people ask me in these recent years, why now? Why, at this specific point, have I chosen to speak up? In some ways, I was already building my island, safe from the mainland. I cannot fully answer that question of why now, for many reasons. From what I know, survivors speaking up and disclosing their truth is by far one of the hardest things we can do. In many cases, we have survived the abuse itself but it is the burden of the shame that we still carry. We carry the trauma in our bodies. We often experience significant physical and mental health issues due to the impacts of the abuse. It feels monumental - if not downright impossible - to shift the shame from ourselves to the abuser, especially when the abuser has often spent many years deliberately destroying our confidence, our self-belief and our self-worth.

When we know better, we should do better. In many ways, I have known better for years. I have known that there was a world outside of my silence. I have known that there is a freedom that comes in speaking my truth. However, there is a difference between knowing and believing.

When I began to deeply believe in what I needed as a survivor I was able to commence building a new foundation. Piece by piece I have created a space for myself outside of the abuse and now I share my story, knowing that it will give someone out there the hope and courage they need to do the same. I am constantly reminding myself that our stories matter and that when we speak our truth and let go of something old, it can open up a little space for something new to be built.

Fifteen

DEAR LITTLE SISTER

I was not expecting to be a big sister. I was eight years old when my sister was born. Eight years is a very long time to be the youngest sibling. In some ways it created a space between myself and this new addition to our family, sending me into the void that middle children often live in. We are not the eldest, the one responsible for all of the firsts. We are not the baby needing all of the extra attention. We sit somewhere in the middle, often forgotten. When I meet people and we discuss our birth order, it is common for people to understand the dynamics and theories about our childhood experiences when it comes to our birth order. Middle children are known to be overshadowed by their older or younger siblings. Phrases like 'middle child syndrome' are common to middle children. We are known for traits such as being the peacemaker, wanting to fit in but also being incredibly independent. I had been the youngest for eight years, and though many children may have been upset that they were no longer the focus of their parent's attention I can safely say that I embraced my role as a big sister wholeheartedly.

Now I will admit, there were moments where I was upset at all of the attention that the baby was getting, and there is even video evidence of me having some irritated moments when I was asked to hand something of mine over to my little sister.

There is a family video which still makes me laugh. We are sitting on the floor in the living room, the video camera on us, and my little sister is sitting upright so she's likely to be over six months at this stage. I am eating a Zooper Dooper, a frozen ice treat, filled with highly sweetened flavours falsely named after fruits. There I was, minding my own business eating my Zooper Dooper when one of my parents asked me to let my little sister try some. I reluctantly hand the Zooper Dooper over, eyeing her suspiciously. Next thing I know her chubby little fingers have grasped the Zooper Dooper, and with her almighty baby grip she refuses to let the plastic tube of grape deliciousness go! I was furious, she couldn't have it, I did not want to part with my Zooper Dooper but I was also aware that my parents would not allow me to snatch it back from her baby death grip. So, I complained, I whined and moaned and my parents tried to appease me by telling me she would not eat much and that she would give it back to me in no time. I was not having it; not only was it my Zooper Dooper but now she had put her slobbery, drooling baby mouth all over it! Yuck! My face glared, I was frustrated and the whole ordeal was captured on camera, forever solidified to remind me that even I, sometimes, did not enjoy having a little sister.

These moments were few and far between. I hope my sister will agree with me but I was and continue to be a pretty amazing big sister. I took my role very seriously and, in many ways, I was like a second mother to my sister from the very beginning. I changed nappies, I fed her, and when we went out on adventures she was always by my side, often being carried on my hip. We were inseparable!

Looking back on my childhood, and even watching other children I have noticed a pattern of when I have been closer to my brother or my sister. There are stages of childhood that are clustered. I see it in my own children. There is the younger children stage, often from birth to when they start school. There is then the primary school to adolescent stage. Next comes the adolescent years and soon after we enter the time of being young adults. Having a brother who was five years older than me and a sister who was eight years younger than me often meant that I was reaching up or reaching down to connect with either of them. None of us lived in each stage of our connection and development with each other for very long. It is comforting these days that we all firmly live in the adult stage, not needing to reach up or down to each other, but all being equals as adults.

When we moved to Queensland from Victoria, I found that my sister and I became even closer. I had lost the connection of the large group of cousins that had surrounded me when I was younger, so I found that my sister and I turned to each other for a deeper family connection. As my brother was 15 when we moved, he was just outside of my reach. In his adolescent stage, I was likely an annoying little sister to him, so it was easier to connect to my little sister and to reach down to her, playing games that she liked and keeping her busy as our parents navigated life in Australia in the early '90s.

Our bond was stronger than ever, and when I look back it is no surprise to me that I made the decisions that I did when the abuse started, the decisions to protect my sister. It did not cross my mind even once that there was any other choice. I had already become her protector in my role as her big sister, so taking a step up to protect her from abuse was something that came naturally to me.

When I look at us today, two adult women, I know that there is so much I have shared with her. I am mindful that the life we have shared together and the bond we have has in many ways been unspoken. An unspoken vow that I made to protect her no matter what, a sacrifice so great that even I did not know how much it would eventually break me.

I have spoken of sacrifice many times. From the human sacrifices of history to the obvious sacrifices I made, ranking my mental health and wellbeing below the safety and childhood experience of my sister. Choosing the idea of family and belonging over myself. In looking back, in seeing how many times the heartbreak of sacrifice nearly broke me I can confidently say that I would do it all again. I would sacrifice it all for my sister, because I know I have gifted her a life that I could have only dreamed of.

When I look at the life my sister has lived, I am incredibly proud of her. Having an eight-year gap between us meant that my parents had worked a few things out when it came to their parenting of my sister. She in many ways got the best of them, and it showed in the educational opportunities she was granted and in the way they parented her. It also showed in where they lived and as she grew it showed in the financial position they were in; they no longer had to support their two older children, as my brother and I both left home in our early adult years.

When I spoke up, telling my father that he was not to touch her, I created a life for her of which I was robbed. No one had been looking out for me, no one had seen the signs of abuse or had even questioned behaviours. But I was watching, not only watching him and listening out for footsteps in the night, I was watching her. I was acutely aware that I could not be with her every second of the day, so it was important for me to also monitor her behaviour and to look for clues that something was not quite right. It was also imperative that I continued to nurture the bond we had, even during my teenage years when the last thing I wanted was to have my little sister hovering around, I knew not to push her away. It was vital to her safety that she saw me as a safe person, soon to be a safe adult, someone she could always turn to if things were not ok.

In a kind of beautiful yet heartbreaking parallel universe, I watched her form a healthy relationship with our father. They were close, she looked up to him like girls often do with their fathers and the bond they had continued to grow as she got older. I watched in amazement as my little sister lived out the life I was meant to live. I watched as she built a father-daughter bond and reaped the benefits of really being loved and safe. I monitored her closely, still looking for signs that something had gone wrong, but they never came. He had listened to me; he understood the boundaries in place and she was free to live her life as his daughter.

Throughout the years I have always been confused by father-daughter relationships. I see girls looking up to their fathers, stars in their eyes. All I see are alarm bells. I find it difficult to trust men, even with their own daughters. I find it difficult to not see them all as a risk to the safety of these young girls.

In seeing my sister and her relationship with our father bloom over the years I have had a front-row seat to what my life could have been. It has been another form of grief, knowing that it was all made possible due to my sacrifice whilst also yearning for the life I could have had. Over the years I have been weighed down by the realisation that her life in some ways was not real, because she did not know the whole truth. She never knew who he really was.

When I disclosed the abuse to my mother and my brother at the age of 16, my sister was eight years old. When our mother did not take us away from our father I had to stay. Maybe out of choice, maybe out of defeat or maybe because I did not know there was any other option. What I do know is that I chose to stay and protect my sister. I have spent almost my entire life choosing to protect her, choosing to keep this ugliness from my sister.

My role as a big sister changed in this choice. Morphing from the expected bond of sisterly love and the simplicity of 'don't mess with my little sister' to becoming an instinctual warrior. My role in her safety was to slay everything that could cause her harm, even if the one I was required to slay was our very own father. I had not slain the dragon in my own story, but there was no way I would make that mistake again.

Over the years I know that there were days where I kept this information about our father away from her to protect her childhood. There were days I saw how much she loved our father and I did not want to ruin that for her. As we both grew there were days that would extend past her childhood, where I would see the woman she had become and how much she valued her sense of family. How much she valued her relationship with our father. There were days where she was convinced that our life was normal and I did not want to take that away from her. That because of my protection, because of my sacrifice and my strength to keep this secret from her that her life was truly normal.

I watched, my heart breaking at times. Longing for the life she had, the life I had helped create for her. I watched as she continued to grow and develop into the woman she is today. My life went on, so did hers.

For over 27 years, from when I was 10 to the age of 37, I see-sawed back and forth, not knowing if I should tell her the truth. She was unaware, living in her own real-life version of The Truman Show.

In the movie, 'The Truman Show', Truman Burbank is a cheerful unsuspecting star of a reality television program. With hidden cameras filming 24 hours a day, Truman lives his life, unaware that everything around him is manufactured. In a world populated by actors, all of them work together with the common goal of preventing Truman from discovering his false reality. In the movie, the creator and producer Christof, who sees himself as Truman's father, is in control of the entire world Truman lives in, directing the actors who play the parts of Truman's family to create a world for him that Truman will never question. In the end, Truman does begin to question his life and realises that the city somehow revolves around him. One night, Truman secretly disappears through a makeshift tunnel in his basement, forcing Christof to temporarily suspend the broadcast for the first time in its history. Christof discovers Truman sailing away from the town of

Seahaven on a small boat. Truman continues to sail until his boat pierces the wall of the dome, the dome which is the television studio his world exists within. Initially horrified, Truman discovers a nearby staircase leading to an exit door. As he contemplates leaving his world, Christof speaks directly to Truman for the first time through a speaker system and tries to persuade him to stay, claiming there is no more truth in the real world than there is in his artificial one, where, although he is manipulated, he is safe. In the very end, Truman makes his decision, exits and the viewers celebrate his escape.

But what comes next for Truman? What exists outside of this man-made life? Outside of the studio dome that is his mainland?

What happens to my sister once she reaches the exit door, and I choose to push her through it?

Dear Little Sister,

I'm sorry. I pushed you out of the door of your reality and exposed you to the truth of the mainland.

I could no longer remain there with you. I had begun to create a new life for myself on my island, but I missed you terribly and could not be at peace in my integrity keeping this secret from you. I could not watch you live your life on the mainland, knowing the lies that it was built on.

The demands of my role to keep you protected from the truth had become too much for me and every day I felt that the toxic truth of our world, the reality of the abuse and the other truths of our father were rotting me at my core.

I'm sorry that I had to turn your life upside down in order to start mine again.

I know you are walking beside me, and your actions since the day I disclosed my truth to you have been nothing short of humbling. It has proven to me that our bond is exactly what I believed it to be; unbreakable. You have proven that the years you spent in the world we created for you and that the sacrifices I made for you have served their purpose. You are and continue to be a woman whose strength and resilience amaze me and I know that together we will come out of this turbulence stronger than ever.

I hope you can forgive me for the hurt you are living through.

I know that one day soon you will find your island, a place where you can be home again. You will have the safety and love that you deserve on your island and you will be able to breathe again, knowing that this new place is really real.

I love you.

Caroline
x

Sixteen

THE YEAR OF FIRSTS

With brave new voyages come uncharted waters. 2020 was the year I embarked upon a new chapter of my life. It was also the year I would find myself catching my breath as everything turned upside down in the world around me as a global pandemic brought us all to our knees. I was starting to build my life on my island and I had no idea what to expect.

At the beginning of this onerous yet liberating year I travelled interstate to meet my sister, to sit with her in person to share my truth and to gently hold her as the world we had created around her crumbled. In what would be a whole new relationship with my little sister

I had to learn to adapt to my new role in her life. In freeing myself of the role I had played for 27 years I was no longer taking on the responsibility of mapping out the world around her. I could finally stop acting, saying goodbye to the scripted role I had played in front of her for all of those years.

She was free to navigate the new world on her own, through her newly opened eyes. Though I would always walk beside her as a support, I was unable to pave the steps ahead of her and I couldn't shield her from what would come next. She would have to walk through this world and experience the minefields. I could no longer protect her in the ways I had previously. I had to stand by and watch the aftermath of my shattering her concepts and beliefs of our family, as she began to form new relationships and ideals.

When I started to build my new world, I had focused my attention on my sister so tightly that I had not seen that I too was required to form new relationships, ideals and boundaries. I had to begin at zero, which in turn came with a year full of firsts.

Many can relate to the concept of the year of firsts. Anyone who is a parent or has watched a baby experience life in their first year will know that everything is new. Every taste, smell and touch are unknown and the sensations and emotions of these firsts can have the tiny human experience a multitude of states, from joy to despair and many other emotions in between. For those of us who have experienced loss and the grief that comes with it, we know too deeply how much these moments of firsts can catch us off guard. For those of us who have been in a long-term relationship and then experienced heartbreak when the relationship comes to an end, what comes next is almost like a sick joke, a comedy of errors as we navigate our post-relationship world. These firsts can come up at any time, even in a moment as simple as visiting your favourite restaurant, a place you and your lost love used to frequent. Being in this space that feels so familiar can be a minefield of emotions as you fit your newly single self into this place that was once shared by the two of you. Now it's a place you sit in alone. This situation can be made worse when the friendly waitress asks, 'Dining alone tonight?' The casual question brings the truth of the private loss out in the open with the awkwardness of what feels like a glaring neon sign. It's a painful reminder that this place used to be shared but now it is different. At this moment you have to feel these feelings for the first time. It may not be the last time you feel them, but the first time can be enough to break you.

This is one of many examples of what a 'first' can feel like after a loss, whilst you are still living within your grief.

I had the benefit of the pandemic, which enforced lockdowns and the distance of being two states away with closed borders when I left the mainland, but my year of firsts when being estranged from my mother continued and I felt each and every moment with the pang of heartbreak and anxiety that sometimes had me bedridden for days.

The pain was in the choice I was making. The choice to stay on my island when I could hear the calls from the mainland trying to lure me back, inviting me to participate in the family calendar moments and milestone events.

To say I felt like the bad guy would be an understatement. The feelings of guilt were palpable when I actively chose not to send my mother a Mother's Day gift. In the weeks leading up to that day I had agonised over the fact that this would be the first year ever that I had not celebrated her and our mother-daughter relationship. I knew I couldn't do both; I couldn't live free on my island and also casually visit the mainland to drop off a gift. It upset me to know I was causing my mother a kind of pain she had not experienced before. A kind of pain that I had not dished out before. But I reminded myself that the pain wasn't mine to carry anymore and that I needed to stay true to my values, respecting what I needed for myself and putting those needs above everything else. Choosing to be Caroline the individual instead of Caroline the dutiful daughter. No longer the good girl.

The firsts hurt and caused a kind of awkwardness as I journeyed through the year, navigating conversations with friends and watching landmark calendar days appear on social media. Watching the world reminded me that most people had what I wanted, but that I could not have those moments without giving up my freedom and the safety of my island. The year rolled on as I navigated Mothers' Days, birthdays and other dates of note, bracing for impact as the days passed me, slowly becoming a little bit better at supporting myself through the moments of grief.

Throughout that year, there was a sense of freedom that grew in me. I knew that the first time for all these things would often be the hardest and that soon I would create a new normal for myself. I knew that speaking about the abuse gave me back my power. A power that now granted me permission to act as I wanted, an opportunity to say goodbye to the old and welcome the new in a year of firsts. I could choose not only what to participate in but also how to participate. I now had the power to live and experience my life in full transparency. I no longer felt the weight of questions that would come if I did not act or participate in the same way I had in the past.

In this new world of transparency, I was free to be and live as me. This year would also be the first time I openly welcomed others to my island and letting people become close to me. During this first year, I celebrated myself and my life by marking out a new set of calendar dates. I began sharing my new home and sharing my island.

Seventeen

MY ISLAND

Have you ever heard your inner child speak? Have you let yourself be vulnerable enough to really tune into their hushed, whispered voice, to really listen to what they are saying? My inner child has repeated clear and specific words to me for most of my life. I have heard these words echoed time and time again. Though I have often ignored her, consciously choosing to silence her, and the words that made me uneasy, they were the words that made the foundations shift under my feet.

The whispered voice of my inner child came to me very clearly; she would say, 'I want to go home.'

It gave me chills hearing that voice. The enormity of what was behind those five simple words. Her longing for safety, her exhaustion from remaining in a place that was dangerous, and reaching for someone, anyone, to take her away.

'I want to go home,' I found myself whispering to myself many times in my life. When I would end up in unsafe spaces with unsafe men. When I was overworked, grinding and hustling to prove my worth to the world. When I would sit at Christmas lunch, smiling for photos and pretending that life was perfect. I wanted so desperately to run away, I wanted so desperately to escape from it all. I wanted to go home.

As we often do with children, I was quick to quiet my inner child. Shushing her and reminding her to look around. 'Weren't we already home?' I said as I pleaded with her to be quiet. Didn't she see the family we had, our parents were here, our siblings were here and we had grown up here, we were married with children of our very own living in this space. We had created a home for ourselves and look at how glorious our life was.

For years I filled my life with more and more accolades. I began creating a life that I could be proud of. I was the mother to two beautiful boys, a proud wife, a successful businesswoman, an advocate for various charities and was constantly proving that I could make a success out of anything to which I turned my attention. Every time my inner child spoke up, any time she questioned our feelings of home, I would add more to my plate, proving more and more how wonderful our life was.

Though I had chosen at the beginning of 2020 to disclose the truth to my sister and speak openly to my parents and my brother about the abuse, I had not realised that in those moments and in the shift from the place I had called home that I would have to create a new home for myself. There were so many things happening all at once that I had seen first-hand, though I hadn't had the opportunity to map out each and every step. There weren't many examples of how this could all play out and when I spoke to others about what I was attempting, about being transparent and my plan to talk about the abuse with my family in person, there didn't seem to be a clear plan forward. I really didn't know what would come of it all.

During the peak of the pandemic, in the various lockdowns that I lived through, I found myself having to create a new sense of home. I now understand that my true sense of home was already in the making. I had been collecting all the elements I needed through all of the years before 2020.

I knew I had to set boundaries and that the home I was creating for myself and my family was a sacred space. I had to protect it as it grew into a stable place, a place where I could live long term. The space was in its infancy, the foundation stones were newly placed and I found it difficult to find the words to describe how important it was to me, how much I needed to protect my precious new home.

The language explaining my new home and what I yearned for came to me in a book, Glennon Doyle's 'Untamed', in a chapter aptly named Islands. It read:

"A woman becomes a responsible parent when she stops being an obedient daughter, when she finally understands that she is creating something different from what her parents created, when she begins to build her island, not to their specifications but to hers. When she finally understands that it is not her duty to convince everyone on her island to accept and respect her and her children, it is her duty to allow onto her island only those who already do and who will walk across the drawbridge as the beloved respectful guests they are. Decide with honour and intention what you will have on your island and what you will not, not **who** *your non-negotiables are but* **what** *they are. Do not lower the drawbridge for anything other than what you have decided is permitted on your island, no matter who is carrying it."*

Since leaving the mainland I have attempted to explain to my siblings why I live on my island. They do not understand because the mainland has always been a safe space for them, as their lived experience of this place is not the same as mine. Since I have disclosed my truth and we have spoken openly as a family they believe the mainland is now safe, they have placed flags to mark out the minefields and as I write these words they still live there, walking through the space in their magical shoes that protect them from the explosions. The closest I can come to the mainland is the shallows of the ocean. They reach for me and ask me to step off my boat, to visit them for a while, to stay for the day in the place I used to call home. But I don't own the magical shoes they are equipped with; I cannot roam the mainland unharmed. I cannot withstand any more explosions. I have to stay away. I have nothing left to give.

In creating my island, I have become a responsible parent, not only to my children, but also to my inner child. The child whose whisper of wanting to go home had become an ear-piercing scream. A cry for help, a desperate plea to be taken somewhere safe where she could be at peace. Both of us needed a safe place to grow, to be free.

When I created my island, surrounded by my husband and our children, I openly welcomed visitors. There were clearly people who could respect the sacred space I had created, honouring the values that I had chosen to build my island on. But the calls from the mainland continued, calling me back and asking me why I would not lower the drawbridge.

By not lowering the drawbridge to my parents I am modelling behaviour to my children that I wish my parents had modelled for me. I am showing them what safety and integrity look like when they are lived. I am showing them that words hold no value if they are not acted out in our truth, if they are not displayed in our lived experiences.

In living on my island with my family I am giving them the gift of me. The gift of my truest, most vulnerable self. The gift of my love.

Most of all, I am giving myself the gift of freedom.

Eighteen

DEAR BIG BROTHER

It's pretty clear that we don't get a choice in our biological family. We are born into this world, through no choice of our own, to the parents who conceived us and into the family who already existed before our first day on earth. Conception can be unplanned, though in some cases our families choose us. I was chosen; by my parents who decided to have another child but, more importantly, by my brother.

I was a wanted child, and from what I know to be true, my brother desperately wanted to be my big brother. He asked my parents to have another child, specifically to give him a little sister. He chose me, he named me and from the moment I was born, he did his very best as my big brother.

That sense of belonging, the intrinsic need for us to belong to something, to belong to our family, is a part of our survival instincts as human beings. Studies of Maslow's Hierarchy of Needs talk about the psychology of this hierarchical pyramid. Yes, we begin with our physiological needs; food, water, shelter and rest, and next, as we move up the pyramid, we require a sense of safety and security. These two elements of the pyramid are classed as basic needs, ones we need as a bare minimum to survive and the ones at the core of our foundation. When we venture higher up the pyramid our needs become psychological; the need to belong and feel loved within intimate relationships and friendships is our third vital need as humans. Once these three core foundations are established, we can then explore further psychological needs around our self-esteem and then go on to meet our personal self-fulfilment needs to reach our full potential.

My captured memories, the endless piles of photos, show my brother and his pride in the role he chose. Looking at the sepia-toned photographs of our life in Mauritius in the early 1980s I can see the tiny baby version of myself cradled by my big brother, staring down at me with a mix of love and nervousness. So desperate to show me how much he loved me, yet so protective and nervous, carefully making sure he is holding me safely, being so conscious of my vulnerability from the very beginning.

Images like these are what I call on when I need to be reminded that I belong to something that is greater than me; something that existed before me and was enriched further in its growth when I was born. Family and love are elements that can continue to grow if they are nurtured and given value. We are automatically connected to each other through our birth, through the blood that links us as family. We are also enriched by the roles we take on, the importance of those roles, and knowing that we have a purpose and someone to belong to.

Knowing how much my brother has worked to show me that I belong is something that warms and breaks my heart all at once. The pride my brother carries is not only for his role as a big brother but also for his place in our family, and for us as a family unit. He has shown such love and admiration for our parents and our little sister. He has been the pioneer for the three of us, and as the children of immigrants, he has paved the way for every challenge ahead.

Being the first is not something he has taken lightly and he has tackled every milestone with a fearless tenacity. Over the years as his little sister, I have watched as my big brother has gone above and beyond to excel in so many areas of his life. He has provided clear pathways for myself and my sister to strive for more, to establish ourselves in our community and to be the best versions of ourselves. He has broken barriers for us in demonstrating what can be done and in stepping out of the mindset of our parents and their generation. In our family, he was the first to be a university graduate, an entrepreneur, a published author, and a thought leader in his community. He has led the way for not only his little sisters but for the next generation to come.

Just as I did not choose to be born into our family, I also did not choose what would come next. Nor did my brother. I did not choose that our father would sexually abuse me and that through his actions my brother would also lose so much, not least of which was his sense of pride in us as a family.

When I think about the reality of my childhood, I know in my heart that my brother could not have protected me from the ugliness that occurred in our home. Whilst he was paving the way for us in many areas of our lives, there was a truth hidden right under his nose that even he could not see. He did not know to listen for the footsteps in the night, he did not know to pick up on the changes in me as I went from a young girl to an abuse survivor overnight. I know for sure that he was not aware of the abuse and I know that when he became aware of it that it broke him. In his desire to create a future life for us, a template for what our lives could be, he could not fix this for us, he could not change the truth.

One thing I can say for sure is that I have had my brother's support and love for my entire life and that the moment I disclosed my truth to him, he believed me. He has always believed me and has always walked beside me, even when he has been torn between being a son and being a brother.

He has supported me, even when I have chosen to no longer live on or visit the mainland. He understands that my choice to no longer visit does not mean that I no longer love him. It simply means that in order to be my best self, I need to live on my island, lowering the drawbridge for him to visit me at any time.

More than one thing can be true, and today I understand that he can choose to be my big brother and also choose to be a son. I understand that even with our physical distance we will always belong to each other. Because we choose to belong.

Dear Big Brother,

Thank you for walking beside me on this journey. I know that you see me as more than what I see myself. I know you see me as more than a survivor, you see a truth and a complexity that is your sister, your little sister who was and will continue to be more than one thing.

I have been torn for some time in my choice to live on my island. It is hard moving away from the mainland where my family has been for all of my life, it is hard making a safe home for myself somewhere new. I wish I could live on the mainland with you, but in addition to not being equipped with the capability to live there safely, there are too many memories that haunt me in that place. I cannot be at peace there, the pain is too raw, the memories trigger me and the trauma still lives on the surface.

I have realised that there has been a struggle for me to understand why you still live there on the mainland, but it recently dawned on me that, similar to more than one thing being true, we can also choose more than one thing. I can see that you are choosing to be a son as well as being a brother, I can see that you are choosing love instead of pain. Our individual choices do not have to mirror each other and I have made peace with my choice to no longer be a daughter whilst also actively choosing to be a sister. I hope you can forgive me for this choice as I know it means coming to terms with the fact that I will never again live with you on the mainland.

Please know that in our differing choices that you are not leaving me behind; you do not need to carry that burden. I know that you choose me, you always have.

You may not need an island of your own, you may have found peace on the mainland as I know that we experience the space in different ways. You are always welcome on my island; the drawbridge is lowered for you. We will always belong to each other and I will always love you.

Caroline

x

Nineteen

FROM VICTIM TO SURVIVOR

I am mindful of how hard I have worked throughout my life to live outside of the abuse. To create a life and legacy for myself that is more than what happened to me when I was a child. I have been curious and entrepreneurial since I was little. It's an enjoyable challenge, always looking for opportunities to get the most out of a situation, finding loopholes or different pathways to find the best and most efficient way of achieving my goals. I am a high achiever; it can be annoying! I can't do things by halves and when I put my mind to something I have a relentlessness that can be exhausting, not only to me but to the people around me.

I often have people ask how I manage to achieve so much in my days. Yes, it is down to hard work and consciously choosing to put the task at hand above and beyond anything else in the day, but it is also a need for control. Being busy and productive is a great form of armour when you are carrying trauma.

I do not call myself a high achiever to gloat; it's not always a good thing. I have watched myself burn out time and time again. I have held on to ideas and roles for far too long when their time has come and gone. I have desperately dug myself into them even deeper, afraid of losing the hours of work already undertaken. Afraid of being a failure, not wanting to lose the armour of that task and the potential of its success, I have invested countless hours striving for perfection and worked tirelessly to prove my value and worth in the world.

There is a fine balance between internally wanting to be successful at something whilst also looking for external validation. My version of best is not always aligned with the outside world, and I have found myself hustling even harder because I have wanted to one-up myself to ensure that what I have delivered and presented to the world would never fall short.

Walking through the world with this mindset whilst also being someone who has experienced childhood sexual abuse has felt like walking on a tightrope. As I have built a public persona, I have been fearful of sharing my story. I am mindful of how hard I have worked throughout my life to live outside of the abuse. To create a life and legacy for myself that is more than what happened to me when I was a child. I have worked so hard to be known for many great things. I have done this because I wanted to do my best, but in many ways, it's because I needed to be known for more than the abuse. This desire was in part to convince the world, but also to convince me. I needed to find a way to ensure that the abuse would not define me.

Sharing my story, whilst knowing how hard I have worked for success feels almost counterintuitive. I've been dancing and performing, trying to hold the attention of the outside world, trying to ensure they only look at the exciting, high-achieving, attractive, shiny things I have to offer. This elaborate parade of successes and wins, with flashing neon signs pointing in many different directions, in hopes that no one would look at the dirty dark underside. That no one would ever find out that I had this ugly truth as part of my story.

The shame of the abuse is in itself complex. It shows up in different ways and impacts me, sometimes when I least expect it. When the shame shows up as an accusation, my inner mean girl can say some pretty horrible things. She tells me that this was all my fault. I can hear her poisonous tone as she tells me how horrible I must be that my own father would do this to me. I can hear her as she demeans my worth and tells me that maybe I deserve this, that maybe I brought this all on myself.

She whispers her nasty words and tells me that when the world finds out about the poison that lives inside of me that all of my hard work and success will come crashing down around me. No one will care about me or respect the work I have achieved; they will only see me as the girl who was abused by her father.

The shame can also present itself externally. I dread the feeling of being pitied. I feel physically ill when I think about people pitying me. The shame turns my perception of the pity I receive from others from their intended sympathy and compassion to a feeling of them belittling me, looking down on me with their pity. I receive pity from others and I warp their well-meaning emotions into my very own feelings of being overwhelmed and embarrassed. The shame turns their pity into my own deep-seated humiliation and I dread the sad looks they will give me as they feel sorry for me. It makes my skin crawl at the thought of their 'poor Caroline' comments. My name in their mouth, saying such sad terrible things. My name connected to something so tragic. I do not want to be seen as weak or damaged. I know these thoughts are also a result of the armour I have worn for so long. Pity means someone cares, and if someone cares then I might need to soften myself, to be vulnerable. Vulnerability is dangerous when the world, or in my case, my family home was so full of trauma.

The high-achieving hustler cannot also be pitied, but we know that more than one thing can be true. As hard as I have tried to create a life for myself despite my childhood sexual abuse for many years, I saw myself as a victim and lived in my own heavy, weighted shame, living in my victim mindset. Though I continued to externally create positive outcomes for myself, though I continued to prove my worth and value to the world, internally, the poison of my victim mindset had me believing that bad things would always continue to happen to me. My victim mindset at its core believed that bad things happened to me because I was bad.

Language is powerful, and the words we choose to speak out loud have the magnitude to change the world. Though it is the words we speak to ourselves, when we quietly whisper or when we tune into our inner voice, those are the words that truly matter.

Before today, in the times I have shared my story, in the moments I have disclosed details of the abuse and the ongoing lived trauma, I have had many people tell me that I am brave, that I am resilient and that I am some kind of hero. The physical sensation I experience at this praise is similar to the discomfort of the pity. I feel a little ill and my body stiffens. I often do not know what to do with those words. I politely thank them for their kindness but internally it is awkward. I did not wish for this, nor did I strive to take on the titles of brave or hero.

I can see that they are attempting to hold a mirror up for me, attempting to help me see my path to resilience. That path is imprinted with my footsteps, each and every step where I have continued to show up, time and time again. The path that has taken me from a victim of childhood sexual abuse to a strong survivor of that abuse.

Today I get to choose who I want to be, I have the power of choice and the power internally to not be destroyed by the traumatic environment that I have lived in for the majority of my life. My bravery cannot exist without my fear, however, and as I share my truth, I am also terrified. The two experiences cannot stand alone. I choose to do what I believe is the right thing, I choose to share my truth, even when it is hard.

The feeling of fright is not the only one that exists as I move away from my victim mindset and enter the space of survivor. There is sadness, an emotion that can see me bedridden for days as I cry, sometimes uncontrollably as my quiet sobs become a howl. A heart-breaking pain that lives in the depths of my very being makes itself heard. A mourning for a life I wish I had, a lived experience that was free from such pain. Though even in these moments, even in the depths of my sorrow, I choose to take steps forward. I choose to be a survivor and I remember when it becomes overwhelming that I can choose to rest, but I cannot stop. There is so much work to be done. Work that I will continue to do, one step at a time.

I remind myself in these moments that it is ok for me not to be ok, that being a survivor in itself cannot happen in a space that is easy. I do not strive for survival from a place where there is no pain; I understand that I survive because I believe that I deserve to exist, that I deserve to live and be the best version of myself *in spite of the pain.*

Moments like these are the days I continue to move further down my path, away from the title of the victim, claiming my survival and walking closer to a place of peace and freedom.

In my choice to no longer be silent about the abuse I understand that I have shifted the focus away from the shining neon signs of my strategic achievements. I have shone a light on the dark underbelly that I could no longer escape. I have acknowledged and come to terms with the fact that I cannot acknowledge and be who I am today without my lived experience. There is no other option but to live this life that I have been given. To acknowledge the trauma, survive it and go on to thrive despite the pain.

In speaking up, in sharing my truth, I remind myself that my words matter, that my story matters, that my truth is mine and it holds a place in the portrait of myself that I have painted for the world. This place in many ways, is just as important as all of my high-flying accolades and achievements.

With the steps of courage imprinted on my journey, I hope that I have paved a safe passage for my fellow survivors. I hope that they can see that they too can step away from being a victim and journey on the path of healing to becoming a survivor. They can build their support network of loved ones, friends and qualified professionals to walk beside them on their journey of healing.

A major driver for me in being as vulnerable as I have been in sharing my truth is that I hope that I have opened the door for others to also break their silence. I want others to find their voice and to know that they can be terrified and brave all at once, just like me.

I want my fellow survivors to know that I am walking beside them.

Twenty

A RIPPLE THAT FEELS
LIKE A TSUNAMI

A sacred space is created when an individual reveals a secret to another. At this moment, two seemingly separate beings find a vulnerability that brings them closer together. In the depths of the moment, there is a bond created between them and they no longer stand on the opposite sides of the line that makes them different. They are united, in their heartbreak, in their strength, in their survival. They share in the survivor's story and sit in a space where they have the opportunity to embrace the empathy at the core of their lived experience.

No two survivors are ever exactly the same, there may be some of you reading my words and hearing my truth that understand elements of my story as they are strikingly similar to your story. Though you know that our experiences cannot be identical, it is the unity, the feeling of not being alone that binds us together. Similar to the need to belong that we have driving us to search for our family, we search for belonging in our survivor brothers and sisters, to enable us to be less alone. Over the years, I have held a special place in my heart for the people who have been brave enough to share their stories. Some I have witnessed share their truth on a stage during a keynote speech and some have looked me in the eyes, holding my hands and whispered the horrible truths of their experiences as we both shed quiet tears together. No delivery of disclosure is greater than another. A keynote on a stage is not any more important than a private discussion. The power is held in the truth and the freedom and the solidarity that comes from sharing our stories.

We know that abuse is born and continues to thrive in silence. The silence is fuel for the behaviour, it punishes the individual by creating the shame that they carry. While that shame grows and forms a heavy weight on the individual, the silence continues to provide a space for the abusive behaviour to thrive, giving the perpetrator further confidence that their behaviour is not only validated but permitted, as no one tells them otherwise. I have lived that experience first-hand; in the silence of the first day of the abuse, there was an opportunity created for my father to continue his behaviour. As the silence continued, he was given more and more power for the abuse to occur and in my case, this went on for four years.

When we create a safe space where we can share our stories, when we live outside of our silence in this safe space, more voices can be heard. The shame can be moved from our shoulders and placed squarely back in the hands of the abusers. The shame is not ours to carry; it is a weapon to silence us and to provide the abusers with more opportunities to use their power for their own benefit. However, I do not suggest this is an easy task for any survivor. Through continued support, survivors can shift the shame. By being clear and open about their abuse they can begin to place the shame exactly where it belongs, with the perpetrator.

In the few years that I have chosen to speak openly about the abuse, I have had many humbling moments where individuals have disclosed their most private pain to me. Some have never spoken to anyone until this point. The moment their words leave the space of silence I see the validation they experience. I know that feeling first hand, but to witness it in another individual is nothing short of inspirational. It takes an immense amount of courage to step out of a place of shame and silence. The words in themselves can feel as though they are too much, or it may even be hard to find the right words, the ones that are enough for a story that holds such a heavy burden. Like the opening of Pandora's Box, sharing the truth about abuse can feel like a world-ending decision.

Similar to the experience of survivors who share their truth, I have spoken with innocent bystanders who grapple with their silence in some ways as much as the survivor has. They carry a burden of what they did or did not do at the time of the abuse. They live in a place of despair when they realise how much damage their silence may have done, how much they may have been complicit in the abuse and what could have been prevented if they had spoken up earlier.

Here we see the damage that can be done, not only to survivors but to the people around them. We see how toxic the space of silence is, as it continues to protect perpetrators, hiding their behaviour in the shadows so it can continue to occur whilst destroying all of the people around them.

In speaking my truth, in sharing my story, I am hoping to create a space that is greater than my individual lived experience. This needs to be about more than just one story. There needs to be a greater good that comes from my human sacrifice. Yet with grand plans such as these, with the real desire to make a change in the world, what feels like a ripple can quickly swallow me whole as it turns into a tsunami.

As I dive into this world, as I open my door to fellow survivors and relive my own personal story, I feel the wave coming straight for me, ready to take me out, burying me underneath the ugliness of this wave of despair and heartbreak. In a way, I have practised for so many years. I use my training as the armour-wearing warrior to push through the wave. I choose to survive knowing that the value of this work is greater than mine. The reality is, as I speak up, others will continue to speak up. I have opened a door for them and I welcome their stories. Even though at times I am overwhelmed by the sheer enormity of how many survivors are out there, I would much rather be overwhelmed by that truth than to know that these truths had been abandoned within the toxic wasteland in the world of silence.

Though it is one of the facts that make me the saddest, I also know that so many survivors are out there currently living in their silence. I know that this experience, that my words, and their words, are all difficult for each and every one of us to hear. But this is where the commonality and our human connection meet. This is where we experience our empathy at its core, where we feel the pain and grief in the story of a survivor and rise in solidarity.

Is all this worth my energy? I have a choice; I can share my truth without being here on the frontline. This experience does not need to be my new sacrifice, replacing one difficult lifestyle with another. I believe that I have chosen to continue to do what I believe is right, even when it is hard. In search of the greater good, I know that there are elements of my story that may not be unique just to me. I know that there are survivors of abuse who are still in the shadows, where the abuse occurred in their homes, at the hands of their own parents. Our stories are somewhat hidden from the public eye. The focus is still skewed to have us believe that the perpetrators are the bad guys we can spot from a mile away. We still look out for the bogeyman under the bed. We still tell our children that there are bad guys *out there*, but we neglect to acknowledge that the bad guy may have sat right next to us at our recent family gathering, or in my case and the case of many others, that the bad guy is also the one that tucks us in at night.

As I watch the ripple turn into a tsunami, as I open my door to my fellow survivors and provide them with a space that is safe for them to be free of their silence, I find strength. I cannot use my voice without acknowledging all I have lost, without using my story to make some kind of change. What I have lost cannot be lost in vain. I see my lived experience as an opportunity to open a space for discussion, not only to the survivors similar to me who need to share their story, but to the rest of the world who need to be educated about this type of abuse and trauma.

I am choosing to share my story of trauma and healing in an attempt to create a safer place, not only for my fellow survivors but for future children who should not have to experience the abuse that we have experienced.

I know that this journey and its incredibly difficult moments are worth my energy because I can already see the change. I can see the way I now show up in the world, how I use my voice to speak up, even when I am uncomfortable, when I use my voice to ensure that I choose safety over politeness. When I use my voice I empower my fellow humans to do the same.

Legacy and intention are important to me. I know what I want to be remembered for. Though I am incredibly proud of the life I have lived so far, I am proud of my family and my other achievements, it is this, today, that I want to be remembered for. I want people to know that I turned my loss into an opportunity for change. I used my voice, even when I was terrified, in hopes that there would be a child out there who would not have to experience a life of trauma similar to mine.

In these thoughts, when I think to myself that it could all be over tomorrow, that one day the tsunami might very well take me out, I will find peace in knowing that what I gave was so much more than what I lost.

Twenty One

ANCESTRAL TRAUMA AND THE NEW GENERATION

Growing up in Australia I often meet people who ask me where I am from. I do not look indigenous, nor do I look English. Where was I born? What is my heritage? This is common for immigrants; people want to know these details but once I share with people that I was born in Mauritius I often get further questions. It seems many people have not heard of this tiny place in the world. Upon further discussion I often receive the remark, 'Why did you leave such a beautiful place?' as people imagine the vibrant blue ocean, white sandy beaches, palm trees and cocktails at fancy resorts. Yes, Mauritius is a beautiful part of the world. Yes, it is now a holidaymaker's dream. But even a place as beautiful as Mauritius can hold some dark secrets.

Even for me, ignorance has been bliss when it comes to the place I was born. I too had bragged about this magical island nestled in the Indian Ocean off the coast of South Africa. As I had not spent much time there as a child, there was a glamourous tourist mentality for me when I spoke about my birthplace. I really did not know much about the history of Mauritius as I had attended school in Australia where Captain Cook was the key historical figure I was taught about.

Unfortunately, just like the tragic history of Australia and the impact colonisation has had on Australian First Nations people, Mauritius holds many ugly truths, which I have discovered have been the starting point for the ancestral trauma that lives in my DNA.

Mauritius does not have First Nations people; the dodo bird was one of the key unique living beings that the island is known for. People did not originally inhabit this space, but due to its location, Mauritius has a thriving history of discovery and tragedy with the earliest confirmed discovery of the island in 1507 by Portuguese sailors. In 1598 the Dutch took possession of the island, later abandoning their efforts to France in 1710. In 1810 the island was seized by Great Britain until it gained its independence in 1968. During these years of various discoverers and possessors, Mauritius was a place where enslaved people were brought from Africa and India. During the 18th century, around 80% of the island's population were enslaved people.

To understand human beings, we often look at data and perform studies to gain a deeper understanding of the impacts of certain factors in our society. It is a numbers game; when we look at the way research data is presented, we are often told that a specific amount of people have participated in a study, a specific amount of people completed a survey or in the case of history that a specific amount of people were impacted by the actions of another group of people. These people are not just numbers, they are the individuals that make up the masses and the individuals that we analyse to further understand ourselves.

Coming from a large family I have been aware of the numbers for quite some time. I am incredibly mindful that if I wanted to, that I could easily gather one hundred Mauritians that I am related to by blood in a room. It wouldn't be too much of a challenge for me to invite them all in and likely know all of them by their first names. If I took the sentimentality out and simply looked at these human beings as research participants, I know I could gather some incredibly interesting data.

If I were to put one hundred people in a room and ask them to complete a survey asking if they had specific health issues, or had experienced abuse, based on the mass of the participant numbers, there would likely be some other people in the room just like me. I know this for a fact simply by talking to a small number of my family members, though I am sure this exercise would make for some interesting discussions and research analysis. It would certainly make for some deep and confronting eye-opening discoveries in just how much we share as family members; just how much we belong to each other in a whole other way.

Similar to the questions around nature versus nurture, I have wondered how much of the negative elements that I have in common with other family members could have been avoided. How much have I experienced due to the environment I have grown up in and how much was outside of my control, passed down through generations?

Until recently I did not understand the devastation of enslavement, nor did I understand that I am likely a descendant of enslaved people. With a recent DNA test telling me I am 49% Indian and 29% African there is a real understanding that my ancestors were likely brought to the island of Mauritius as enslaved people. Knowing that they existed in this place against their will breaks my heart.

Though I am a proud Creole Mauritian woman, I am mindful that the Creole people of Mauritius today remain among the poorest and most disadvantaged in Mauritian society. I am not surprised that my parents moved us to Australia in the hopes of breaking cycles in an attempt to provide myself and my siblings with new opportunities. What saddens me is how we have been unable to escape the trauma of our ancestors. The trauma has continued to live with us, carried in our DNA.

There is various research around the legacy of trauma and if it can be passed down to future generations. Studies have shown that trauma can cause mutations to our genetic code, changing the way DNA is expressed and how that change can be passed down to the next generation. This process of epigenetics is where genes are modified without changing the DNA code itself. Tiny chemical tags are added or removed from our DNA in response to changes in the environment in which we are living. These tags turn genes on or off, offering a way of adapting to changing conditions without inflicting a more permanent shift in our genomes.

The consequences of passing down the effects of trauma are astronomical, even if they are seemingly subtly altered between generations. It changes how we view our lives in the context of our parents' experience, influencing our physiology and even our mental health.

Knowing that the consequences of our own actions and experiences now could affect the lives of our children, even long before they might be conceived, could put a very different spin on how we choose to live. Epigenetics is thought to be the link between nature and nurture, where a persons' experience alters how their DNA is read by their cells.

This research saddens me, but in many ways does not surprise me. In my journey as a survivor, I have been conscious that trauma cannot exist in a vacuum. It is not lost on me that I have been diagnosed with chronic fatigue, an autoimmune disease. From my understanding the only other family member I am aware of that also has this disease is my father. The trauma lives in our DNA and just as we are linked by the trauma, we are also linked by the symptoms it causes. Our bodies keep reminding us of this. Our experiences impact the people around us significantly, I know this to be true as I have seen first-hand how much I have changed due to the trauma I have experienced. Though I do not ever excuse the actions of a perpetrator it is important to acknowledge the likelihood that they have experienced trauma and abuse of their own, be it first-hand or passed down from previous generations.

Being a parent, it frightens me to know that I may have already inadvertently passed on my traumatic experiences to my children in their DNA. I have pro-actively been working on breaking cycles of abuse and raising my sons to be safe men in the world.

Unfortunately, we are still living in a 'boys will be boys' world, where men who carry the trauma of their past, whether they are abuse survivors themselves or simply have altered elements in their DNA, go on to cause abuse and trauma. These men are not held accountable, nor are they offered any mental health or trauma support. We simply label them as good or bad.

Nothing can be done to change this cycle of abuse, be it at the DNA cellular level or as we walk amongst each other through this world, if we do not start holding each and every individual accountable for their actions and start demanding change. The healing journey for survivors can be staggered or completely derailed when the perpetrators are not held accountable. There is no real apology, no 'sorry' worth accepting without real change.

When we look at survivors who may also be perpetrators, we must remember that they are also independent to the people around them. Regardless of whether they have experienced abuse themselves or have simply chosen to do harm, they must be the first to want to make a change and break the cycles of further trauma. They are independent, an individual with choice; no one can do the work for them and at times the criminal justice system cannot be the only answer. There needs to be different versions of 'better'. When we know better, we need to actively do better.

The science of epigenetic inheritance and the effect of trauma is still young, which means it is still generating heated debate. Where researchers are with epigenetics is similar to how it was when researchers began investigating PTSD. At the time it was a controversial diagnosis, as not everyone believed there could be long-term effects of trauma. Nearly 30 years later, PTSD is a medically accepted condition that explains why the legacy and impacts of trauma can span decades in a person's lifetime.

Based on the research, it is shown that subjects can unlearn the associations of trauma triggers and the pain associated with those triggers, which implies that the next generation may be able to escape the effects of the trauma. This research also suggests that if humans inherit trauma in similar ways, the adverse effect on our DNA could be undone using techniques like cognitive behavioural therapy. There's a malleability to the system, a neuroplasticity, the template isn't set in stone and by healing our trauma we can put a stop to it impacting our future generations.

Twenty Two

LIFE OUTSIDE OF SILENCE

Coming from such a large family, with my 28 first cousins and who knows how many more second and third cousins, I have found that living in this new world, outside of my silence, has its challenges. The abuse that I experienced and the continued trauma that I lived through isn't easy to talk about, let alone something I would bring up over a casual barbeque lunch in my backyard. Even though I actively live in a place on my island where I am no longer silent about the abuse and about my survival, I am equally mindful of how uncomfortable people find this subject matter. My story can trigger people, particularly if they are fellow survivors, but I've discovered that it can also trigger people who haven't experienced abuse. For the people that see themselves as bystanders, my story can make them uneasy as they second-guess their own decisions in their lives. They may think back to times where they may have chosen politeness over their instincts, in a moment when something was not quite right.

Since my childhood, there has been an unspoken understanding regarding my father when it comes to specific family members. I know that many of them are aware of his behaviour, though prior to 2020 I don't believe many of them knew that his behaviour had impacted me, or that I was one of the survivors of his violations. In some instances, family members have spoken to my father directly about his behaviour. Unfortunately, though, in many cases family members have ignored his behaviour, choosing politeness over instinct. Choosing the bliss of ignorance over the courage of doing what is right has been more comfortable for them than rocking the boat of the social status quo.

In my attempt to strengthen my voice, to find confidence in sharing my truth and in really knowing that my story can help others I have found ways of sharing my story through different mediums.

In 2020, I launched a podcast. During the introductory episode, I chose to state for the first time to a broad audience that I am a survivor of childhood sexual abuse.

It was a relatively subtle moment, a two-second piece of audio delivered in the context of a number of other Caroline facts, but it was there, permanently out in the public for anyone to hear, if they chose to really listen.

I was terrified when I released that episode. I had actively supported charities in this area publicly and had spoken to friends in private about my lived experience, but this was the first time I'd revealed myself as a survivor in a public arena. I was worried that this information would upset people, namely my extended family members. I was concerned that people in our family would be worried about our reputation and our family name or that I was drawing attention to myself and my family in a negative way. Those feelings of dread haunted me for weeks, bubbling away in the depths of my stomach, making me nervous and anxious. Every time the phone would ring, I would think to myself, will today be the day that someone calls and yells at me? It was a fear that was almost childlike, the fear of being reprimanded. It was akin to the feelings of apprehension I remember feeling when I was younger and was disciplined by an older family member who believed I had done something wrong.

The podcast was released in August and as it was an interview format to share the stories of inspirational women, I quickly disregarded the nerves that came from my introduction episode. I began focusing on the interviews to come, the production of the podcast and how to get these stories out to the world. Being action-focused meant that I could easily turn my attention to the things that didn't need to be about me and I could carry on creating wonderful episodes and sharing incredible stories.

Like most things in my life, the podcast sat on my list of things to do, amongst various other projects and tasks. I keep chipping away at releasing weekly episodes to the world and in many ways, I almost forgot that I had spoken of being a survivor of childhood sexual abuse; the moment had come and gone and I moved on to the next thing.

Looking back on what was to come next, I really shouldn't have been surprised. I know now that sometimes the most important conversations are the ones you don't expect. The impact you can have on people at times spring from the actions you don't plan. They happen in the moment, when you feel into them, when you have to be vulnerable and simply let yourself go.

My phone rang on an early November morning of 2020. I recognised the name, one of my uncles, one that I barely spoke to, but I still had his number saved in my phone. I answered reluctantly, conscious that I was in the middle of my work day, but curious as this was not a person who would ever call me. The usual small talk occurred, his vibrant personality larger than life, something, on reflection, that I've always questioned about him. He had always been that family member who was a little left of centre. I had been told to steer clear of him as a child and there was a part of me that had always wondered why his personality was so large and why he was always pushed to the edges of our greater family. As he started to speak my initial thoughts were, 'What does he want and why on earth has he called me?'

My uncle explained that I had popped up on Facebook as someone the social media platform suggested he should connect with. We have various mutual friends on the platform and as he looked at my profile, which is relatively locked down through my privacy settings, there were only a few items he could see, one of which was the link to my podcast. He'd clicked on the link and listened to the first episode, my introduction episode.

The words that only took me two seconds to speak were all that he needed to hear to pick up the phone and call me. Life outside of silence had opened a door, to a man who was my uncle, to a man who was also, as it turned out, a survivor.

Over the course of a three-hour phone call, he spoke openly to me. He shared his truth about being sexually abused by one of his brothers, one of my other uncles.

He shared stories of other abuse in our family, both at his generational level, as well as mine, and he cried as he thanked me for believing him and for holding a safe space as he spoke his truth. He shared with me that in his 60 years of life not once had a family member given him a safe space to share, nor had they really understood the enormity of the weight he had been carrying all his life. When I think of the complexities of his truth, that my uncle comes from a generation where abuse survivors were not believed and where men never disclosed their pain, it filled me with sadness. The shame of the abuse was greater than any perceived benefit of disclosing it. During our call, as he related what had happened to him, and still today, I am filled with so much pain at the reality of this truth. I wept when he shared that sense of shame with me. I have carried my truth for nearly 30 years; I do not know how I could multiply that weight, times it by two, and continue to function in the world.

We talked about the abuse I had experienced as a child. Even though he had his own stories to share and had been living in his darkness and heartbreak for over 60 years, he still experienced a deep shock hearing my truth. We spoke about many things. But this unexpected connection was the real beginning of my understanding of the ancestral trauma that lives in our family, the damage that has been done and the real opportunity we have to make a change in this space for our children and the next generations to come.

Over the next few days after this initial phone call, my uncle reached out to other family members, expressing his concerns, sharing parts of both of our stories in the hope of there being some kind of accountability and action. Some of the family members he spoke with had never heard about the abuse I had experienced. When I realised he had done this, I initially went into shock. This was no small moment in time and as I have always worked so hard to be in control of my story and who I share it with, this was a moment where my words were taken out of my hands and placed in front of a far larger audience. I had been clear to my uncle that there was no silence required, that he was free to share my truth with whoever he chose to, but as things moved so rapidly there was little time to catch my breath. I realised that he had been the ripple that was needed to cause another tsunami. He was the new voice I needed to share initial parts of my story so I could go on to have the larger discussions.

That first moment, when the stark words, 'Did you know that Caroline was sexually abused by her father?' left his mouth and landed on the ears of family members represented some of the hardest words to speak out loud to the ones we love. Though my uncle spoke those words, I was aware that it was me speaking my truth, and that was the beginning of this new wave of truth-telling. There is a poison that escapes when the truth is told and it is terrifying being the one who speaks these words, knowing how much damage they can do, knowing how much they can shatter the illusion of what everyone has believed until this point in time.

Similar to my sister living in her own version of 'The Truman Show' prior to me disclosing to her in February of 2020, in these weeks of November 2020 I realised there were so many family members and loved ones that lived a similar existence to her. So many that we were acting for, so they could all continue to believe that everything was perfect.

Once my uncle created the ripple, I quickly felt the effects of the tsunami. My phone rang for weeks with uncles, aunts and cousins reaching out to hear the truth from me directly. They wanted to ask questions, and to attempt to get their heads around how complicated and devastating this truth was.

This experience of reliving the abuse over and over again, of sharing my truth of what my father had done, with people that loved him, was soul destroying. With every phone call, every discussion, every single text message, I was tense, waiting for someone to turn on me. I was waiting to have someone tell me to be quiet or that they no longer wanted to associate with me because I had ruined our family name. Yes, even with all of the work I had done internally, the emotional and psychological journey I had been on and by me moving away to the safety of my island, it was still not enough to quiet the internal voice of the mean girl who could easily convince me that I was risking too much, that I would be the human sacrifice again.

I remember a day when my entire body went into shock, as one of my closest family members had heard the truth and I was genuinely waiting for him to turn his back on me. My brain wanted to power through that specific day, so I attempted to make plans to meet friends for lunch and distract myself once I was made aware that he now knew. My body had a very different idea and began to shut down. I was sitting at the dining table drinking a cup of tea and I started losing my vision, seeing black spots and feeling lightheaded. I felt literally sick with apprehension. My hands started to shake, I almost dropped my tea and I struggled to catch my breath. I began to hyperventilate, cold chills running all over my body as I went into a full state of shock. I rushed to my bedroom, crawled under the covers and asked my husband to cancel all of my plans for that day. Wrapping myself up in my blankets like a safe cocoon, I slept for the remainder of the day until my body calmed and regulated itself again.

I'll never forget that day, that feeling of losing control, that feeling when the tsunami was ready to take me out as the mean girl in my head screamed all of the nastiest things she could say on a megaphone.

I'm grateful to say that this close family member did not, in fact, turn his back on me. He contacted me and spoke with nothing but love and support and has continued to provide me with support in the ways that he can. I haven't really lost anyone to date. That does not mean that the drawbridge to my island is open to anyone that I am related to by blood. There are many people who have not reached out, or who I know would have made similar choices to my mother in their complicity. They are not welcome on my island. These are the people I have distanced myself from. My island is a safe place and holds very clear boundaries; the drawbridge isn't lowered for my parents, nor is it lowered for anyone else who may not live the values that I hold firmly in place.

Being from such a large family I know there will be family members that may read my words and hear these stories for the first time, be it my story, or the story of my uncle. What I've learned from this experience is that the more we speak our truth the more we can control the narrative. No one can tell my story quite like me, and though I appreciate the moments where someone else can speak the first few words, providing me with some reprieve from always having to be on the front line, there is an act of real courage that comes from speaking our truth.

It is incredibly nerve-wracking being out here in the world without the armour of my silence. There are days where I miss the carefully scripted role I played as I acted like everything was ok. In this new space, though, I am proud that I find the courage to show up every day outside of the silence. I am still working out who I am today, what I do next and how this new world can be a safer place for all of us. This is a lived experience, an ongoing journey that I take step by step, each and every day. I am proud to walk beside my fellow survivors and I will forever be grateful to my uncle who picked up the phone and honestly shared his truth with me. Because despite what we have lived through, we are still here. We are survivors of our collective trauma and we are the heroes of our own stories.

In the words of Darius Simpson, 'We are our ancestors' wildest dreams.'

Twenty Three

DEAR LITTLE CAROLINE

In April 2021 I sat in a room with my parents for the first time since I disclosed the abuse to my sister in 2020 and since I chose estrangement. My siblings were there too; it was the first time we had all been in a room together in nearly two years.

Sometimes I think about these moments of courage, where I have shown up time after time, in the face of my fears and thought that I must be absolutely out of my mind. Deep in my moments of fear, there lives a flame of hope fuelling the fire of my courage. I'm also very mindful that if I want to make a change then I need to do things differently, even if that means facing my fears head-on.

To clarify, my parents aren't scary; they are loving, charming, well-mannered human beings. Yes, like anyone, they have their moments of anger and sadness, which I witnessed on this particular day, but I am not afraid of them. The fear I speak about is different to the fear I would likely experience if I felt my physical safety was in jeopardy. I do not fear that my father will sexually abuse me again; I am a grown woman, and though he may still have some strength in his old body, I have my mental and physical strength that gives me confidence in my safety.

This fear is a combination of many things. Sometimes the fear is fuelled by the mean girl within who tells me that my parents are going to blame me, that they are going to yell at me in front of my siblings and tell me that I have ruined our family. Sometimes my fear is at the hurt I know this situation causes us all, especially my siblings and being fearful of having to sit in that hurt, having to witness it first-hand. But most of all the fear comes from a deeper place, one where my younger self, my inner child, is scared. In the purity of the innocence of my inner child also sits the real fear that I experienced when I was a child and my father would come into my room at night. These were the moments when my body would freeze and my words would be trapped inside of me. That is a fear I have carried almost my entire life. There are nightmares

I haven't been able to shake and though I am actively seeking professional support to shift these disturbing visions and triggers, I am conscious that these nightmares may remain with me for the rest of my life.

That moment, sitting in the room with my family, I had the opportunity to speak for myself, with my parents and my siblings all as witnesses so my words could not be misconstrued. What I didn't know is that this would be the day that I would carry my inner child with me, this would be the day my inner child would find her voice, transporting her trapped words, speaking them through the clear voice of her now 38-year-old self.

I felt her with me on that day, 10-year-old Caroline, 11, 12, 13, 14, 15, and 16-year-old Caroline. It was like in a split-second I could see her standing with me in the room, my 38-year-old self, standing in front of a collection of mini-Carolines, shielding them as I have done for all of these years. In this moment, each and every past version of myself had been given a key, they had unlocked each door and had all stepped out simultaneously, ready to stand tall, ready to no longer hide in the darkness of shame and silence, ready to speak, through me.

I have spent my entire life putting myself and the versions of me into boxes, boxes behind walls, boxes inside of boxes. All to protect myself from further hurt and disappointment. Releasing Caroline, every version of her on that day, has given me the freedom to be whole again. I am no longer divided, boxes inside of boxes. I am one fully formed being, fully formed in my truth.

In this truth I too can be more than one thing. I can be a survivor and still find joy in my life. I can let my inner child explore the freedom of her innocence, no longer trapped in fear. I can be serious and silly. I can be free.

On that day, when I looked at my father, I explained to him that I did not have a voice when I was 10, but that I was holding the younger versions of myself and speaking on their behalf. I explained to him that what he did has caused me significant emotional and physical pain, and that everything that happened was wrong and that it was his fault. In that moment I spoke for her, I found her voice from that very first night when the abuse started, her voice that had been hidden under the darkness of the shame he had shadowed us in. I found her voice and placed it safely back in her hands. It is hers to keep; her voice, her innocence, her freedom. Today at this very moment, with my shoulders back and my head held high, I am ready to speak for them. There is no quiver in my voice. I speak our truth and I share our words with conviction. I will continue to stand guard in front of the army of my younger selves, and they can live in the safety of knowing that no-one will ever take our voices away from us again.

Dear Little Caroline,

I'm so sorry. I never wanted to lock you away for so many years. There was such a fog in the space where you were trapped, a darkness where you not only lost your voice but had to remain in fear. I'm sorry that in protecting you that I had to force you to lose so much of yourself, so many moments of your life as a 10-year-old and further years of loss to come.

In all of the sacrifices you have made for us, I have found strength; each sacrifice made was not lost in vain. Today I have found our lost voices, and I have spoken up for us and shared our truth. The shame that created the darkness is lifting, and though some days may be hard and we may revert back to the place we used to live in to seek safety, I can promise you that I am fighting and will continue to fight for our freedom in our truth.

I am sharing our story so that everything we have sacrificed does not go to waste. We are making a difference in this world and I want to remind you that even when you have nightmares and feel afraid, it is not your fault.

Please find peace in knowing that you no longer have to listen for footsteps in the night, you no longer have to keep secrets, no one is coming to hurt us. I am here to protect us, each and every one of us.

Did you know we have an island now? I have built a home for us, one of our very own. Our island is beautiful and we are surrounded by so much love, we are finally safe.

I can't thank you enough for choosing to survive, I'm so proud of you and hope that you know that your words are safe with me. No one will ever take that safety away from us again.

I love you little one, go and enjoy your freedom, you deserve it.

Caroline

x

Twenty Four

MY FATHER, IT'S TIME TO SAY GOODBYE

The trauma I experienced shows society has a vastly inaccurate image of who perpetrators actually are. We are taught that they are monsters that are easy to spot, or that they are hideous creatures, like the bogeyman that we feared as children. We are taught that when we spot them, we should shriek and point so everyone else can be safe too and we imagine grabbing our torches and pitchforks to hunt down the monster if he dares to cause harm so that we can easily slay him and make our community safe again.

So, what do I do when the monster isn't the hulking troll under the bridge but lives in my own home, provides me with a place to live, puts food on the table, teaches me about art, shares music with me and provides me with some of the core values I still hold to this very day? How do I slay the monster when he is the charming man that is also my father?

I've always wondered if people notice that I do not speak about my parents much, or more specifically if people notice that I do not speak about my father. I soon realise that as human beings we are often more preoccupied with ourselves and our loved ones to realise that someone's reality may be vastly different to our own. This comes up for me at key dates in the year, the hardest being Father's Day when my social media feed is filled with friends and family telling me how wonderful their fathers are. They delight in honouring their hero dads and celebrating the beautiful relationships they share. These moments of celebration often extend even further into their family, into the older generations when I see photos of generations of men celebrated by the people in their lives. Fathers with fathers being glorified and acknowledged for all of the good they have done for their families. The connection they have is admired, along with the way they belong to each other.

I have always found myself deeply uncomfortable when I see women and girls talk about their relationships with their fathers. As I've grown, this sense of discomfort moves me to take a step back to observing with curiosity. If they are grown women this observation can often fill me with sadness, a longing for what they have, and a longing for a relationship I said goodbye to so many years ago. I wonder to myself what that must feel like, to have a relationship with your father and to feel safe in his presence, and in turn to be able to give that feeling of safety to your children so they too can have a relationship with this father figure, so they can feel a sense of belonging and paternal connection.

If I am watching a young girl with her father a darkness can overshadow me and my protective instincts kick in. I begin to feel tense. I find myself trying not to stare at them but not wanting to look away. My lived experience tells me that fathers are not always safe men. Alarm bells ring loudly in my ears. My eyes scan for signs of something wrong, the slightest discomfort of the young girl often sending my mind to dark places where I suspect the worst must be happening in their home at night. Maybe she too has to listen for footsteps. My body becomes rigid, not really knowing what I would actually do if I did see any of those clues. Not knowing if the flight instinct would see me turn away or the fight reaction would see me step in to ask questions. This is an exhausting experience, a hypervigilance that I carry in my body. There is no way to relax as the trauma inside of me is triggered by these unassuming strangers. I have to rationalise with my trauma brain to 'calm down', to not think the worst of everyone and to simply enjoy the wonder that is a father with his daughter, creating positive memories one moment at a time. It's a balancing act, this process of quieting the alarm bells whilst also tuning in to my instincts.

In many ways, I'm not surprised by the vast difference between our perceived image of perpetrators compared to who we know them to really be. The statistics exist, and we do not need to look too hard to find them. We know that 17% of women and 4% of men are sexually abused before the age of 15, and of those numbers, only 11% are sexually abused by strangers.

I was personally surprised and saddened to learn that 13% of children sexually abused were abused by their fathers or step fathers. Learning this helped me feel less alone, but in turn also made me feel incredibly sad for the many people out there with lived experiences similar to mine. I have never wished for anyone to experience the pain and shame I have carried for so many years.

With statistics like these so easily accessible it surprises me that many people still believe they will easily be able to spot a perpetrator, that the image of the monster still exists in their minds. We know that perpetrators select their victim-survivors as targets due to the ease of grooming them and their caregivers. Grooming is manipulative behaviour that the abuser uses to gain access to potential victims. At times predatory behaviour can be opportunistic, in the case of perpetrators having access to victims due to children being left in their care.

This fact of how often opportunistic behaviour occurs became even more apparent to me when I recently connected with Aishah Shahidah Simmons after hearing her speak in an interview held by the "Me Too" movement. Aishah shares her story publicly of the abuse she endured at the hands of her paternal step-grandfather whilst in his care, as her parents travelled for work. She went on to live a lifetime of trauma as her family kept the abuse a secret, expecting her to live in their family unit, often still in the home she was abused in, whilst carrying the enormity of this secret.

When I heard Aishah's story I wept. Her experience is so similar to mine that I felt a sense of relief in a way, knowing that I was not alone and that there may be a pathway for me to follow to find peace. As I connected with Aishah further I discovered her anthology, *Love with Accountability, Digging up the Roots of Child Sexual Abuse*. In reading the collection of voices and experiences I found an even deeper understanding of how prevalent this issue of child sexual abuse is within families, which in turn helped me further understand my own confusion around how to seek justice.

I am constantly torn between the advice I am given to seek legal justice, whilst also not fully believing that the legal system can make real change in this space. I am not convinced that incarcerating perpetrators is the answer, though I don't expect all survivors to agree with me nor do I have a plan forward as to what to do next.

If we go back to the statistics and think about how many perpetrators walk among us every day, we simply do not have the space in our criminal justice system to convict them all. Even if we did, is it possible to rehabilitate them, and if so, how? How do they serve their time and receive psychological support to really change their behaviour so our children can be safe?

Then we have the scale of abuse itself. We see time and time again crimes where men violently rape women and are freed from our incarceration system once they have served their time. If men who are causing this type of violent harm are being released, then what do we do with the preparators that are acting in ways that sit far lower on the abuse scale? We know that an inappropriate touch can escalate to something more each and every time a perpetrator gets away with their behaviour, so how do we intervene and stop the behaviour for good?

I don't have the answers. I wish I did. My feelings on this topic bounce from sadness to rage as I wish for answers that are easy to implement. But if I, a survivor of my father, cannot decide what to do with him, how do we collectively as a society decide what to do with all of the other perpetrators? Men that are more than one thing, men who do good, who are good and yet are also the monsters we fear?

Father,

This may be one of the last times I say goodbye to you. I know there will come a day where you no longer walk on this earth and I will need to say goodbye for the last time, but between now and then there are many days to come. I don't know what the days in between today and your last will hold, but what I do know is that in many ways I have been saying goodbye to you, to us, for many years.

I miss you; I miss the parts of you that are good. I miss the parts of you that I called Dad. I miss the parts of you that I truly loved.

In the same way, I miss those parts of you I know that I carry with me. I carry them like a tragic love story, where there is joy and heartbreak all at once.

What you took away from me, from us, is something that I can never forgive. Because not only did you take something away but you replaced it with something so poisonous that I've struggled to heal myself since that very first day you inflicted it upon me.

I hope you find a way to heal yourself, as I know there is a poison that lives in you too.

I cannot keep carrying this poison, and I will not pass it on to my children, so today I have to let it go.

I have to say goodbye.

Caroline

Twenty Five

ARMOUR, SHAME AND SOFT CENTRES

As I have locked away memories of the abuse and trauma, I have also struggled to limit these protective force fields to only the small amount of harm-doers in my life. Rather, I've applied them sweepingly, casting a wide net and gathering up every memory I could, to protect myself from the pain of the truth. In locking myself away, in protecting myself, I have for many years stopped the majority of people that want to connect with me from getting too close. I have disconnected from the world and created a barrier between myself and my loved ones.

At times these protection mechanisms were designed not only to protect me but also to numb and deflect pain. As I shared from my teenage years I have numbed with drugs and alcohol and engaged in problematic relationships. The armour has deflected all emotions at times, sacrificing real happiness and joy as the armour I have put in place has not had the capability to pick and choose which emotions are safe and which are not, so all are deflected.

Masks and acting have created moments where I have pretended that everything is fine, sometimes genuinely convincing myself, which led to additional unsafe spaces with unsafe men. It has been dangerous when the masks and the acting have caused me to not recognise myself, each layer shinier than the next, each scripted line another lie to convince myself that everything was ok.

In addition to living and believing the lie, multiple versions of myself were created. They all served a purpose and the shiny masks mirrored what I believed people wanted me to be. The good daughter, the good sister, the good wife, the good mother, the good friend, the list of 'good Carolines' goes on.

Why only good? There was no room for a bad Caroline on the outside as so much poison and ugliness already existed on the inside. Bad Caroline was dangerous, reckless with her body and catastrophic to her mental health. Only good Caroline was allowed to exist; no shades of grey. I only existed on one end of the scale or the other, there was no in between.

Over the years as I continued to hide behind the various layers of protection, I convinced myself that my life and the way I displayed it on the outside was real. I convinced myself that I really did have it all together and that the version the outside world could see was the real version of me. All the while, I knew there was so much more underneath the layers and so much more to life that I was missing. The people who constantly attempted to get close to me knew they were missing out too; they could never really get close enough, they could never really know the real Caroline.

There were and continue to be so many detrimental effects of this armour. The way that it has not been selective in who it has kept away, many times upsetting the people I love the most. The way that it has isolated me and kept me in my silence, hiding secrets for decades. The way that it has hidden my truth, inadvertently protecting people and actions that should not be protected.

I had to question the entire process, the entire way that I was choosing to layer myself. In disabling my armour, putting down the masks, ripping up the script, stepping out of the boxes and out from behind the walls, I realised that all of those words, each and every one of them were words that could easily be renamed as shame. Every single layer was shame.

It dawned on me that all of these words had been distracting me from the reality of the shame. When I picked up the shame and placed it squarely back where it belonged, back in the hands of the perpetrator, I did not need to hide behind the shame anymore. It was never there to protect me; it was there to silence me, to protect the perpetrator.

The armour I've been wearing, carrying such a heavy burden of shame, was designed to weigh me down and convince me that I needed it to survive living in a battlefield. In leaving the mainland, in no longer having to withstand the explosions of that unsafe and traumatic place, I no longer need to be in battle. I am not a warrior constantly on the lookout for the next explosion ready to destroy me. I am a woman who is finding a sense of peace. I am a woman who knows that the softness of my inner self is the part of me that has the most to give.

By disabling my armour and the other mechanisms I've known and relied on for so many years I have had to create a new way of living. Yes, my island is now the place where I live, the place where I can connect with my loved ones, but it takes daily practice to not fall back into previously modelled behaviours. It can be easier to pick up the script when I've played a role for so long.

I do not know who this version of me is at times. I'm still learning how to live in the grey space of life, where failures happen, emotions are complex and there is space in between good and bad. It takes showing up and trusting myself, a choice that I commit to every day.

It takes a strength, yet also a softness to be vulnerable enough to let people in and to share my life with them. I now choose to show the people I love my true self and to really love them in a way that can only be done without shame and without barriers between us. In the messy middle of life, I am more than one thing and can experience joy and sorrow in the safety and shelter of my island.

Twenty Six

DEAR HUSBAND

Putting aside different spiritual and religious beliefs, while I understand that we technically have one life, I have often spoken to people about the multiple lives that I have lived.

Many times, I've heard people describe the diversity of their careers as having lived multiple lives. For me, personally, I could say in a previous life I worked for the Queensland Police Service at their training academy, I worked as a receptionist at a hair and beauty salon in London, I worked as an administrative assistant at the Tate Gallery in London and I also worked in the shipping industry as an exports account manager, and these are just some of the roles I've had. In addition to that I've spent the majority of my life being an event manager, and more recently being the founder of a lifestyle management company.

These are just my different career paths; when I say that I've had previous lives I also refer to my personal life. I met my now ex-husband when I was young and by my mid-twenties, we had lived overseas together, purchased property, got engaged, had a baby, got married and purchased a business together. When I look at that list of achievements, I'm amazed that all of that happened in such a short period of time, but then I'm also not surprised. A lot can happen in seven and a half years. But, due to some things out of my control and some that I take full responsibility for, our marriage was not to be. In my late twenties, I found myself divorced, but in true Caroline style I was quickly moving on with a new partner, in a new city, ready for a new life.

So, by the time I turned 30 I was in my second marriage, had my second child, and was well and truly embedded in another life, the one I hope to stay in for many years to come.

I won't claim that going through a divorce with very difficult circumstances whilst attempting to raise my first-born son plus start a new relationship was easy. Divorce is hard. It requires you to start again and during the experience, even if, like me, you initiate the divorce it still comes with heartbreak and grief as the world you chose and believed would be forever comes crumbling down around you. I recall being challenged time and time again by well-meaning family members about my choice to end my marriage, and then further questions came regarding my choice to start a new relationship. But one thing stood out to me that seemed to be the shift that I had been searching for most of my life. I wanted to be the best version of myself, I wanted to feel at home in myself and I knew that in my first marriage that simply wasn't possible.

Reflecting on that feeling, the distance between who I was as a child, who I was in my first marriage and who I am today, I would be naïve to disregard the importance of the safety I have needed within the relationships in my life. When we have safety, one of the core foundations of our human needs, we can then enter the space of love and belonging, moving then to our space of esteem and then self-actualisation. I didn't have this language when I chose to leave my marriage but I knew somewhere in myself that I needed to find safety in my closest relationships so I could be the best version of myself.

As I continued to be questioned by family members, and more importantly by my son, who was grappling for answers as to why his parents were now divorced and why I had left his father, I simply answered, I need to be the best version of myself; once I'm the best version of myself I can be the best mother to you. I know I can't do that if I stay in this marriage.

Looking at where I stand today, on my island, the core of my decision making is the same. I can't be the best version of myself if I stay on the mainland, I can't grow and be free if I stay in relationships that do not bring out the best in me. So, in the same heartbreaking way that I ended my first marriage, I have chosen to live on my island, away from my family.

I recently attended a Dare to Lead Leadership Program, developed by Dr Brené Brown and facilitated by Kemi Nekvapil. During the program, we were asked to write the names of the people whose opinions really matter to us within a square on the page in our workbooks. The workbook was the usual A4 sized book, but the square was small, measuring no more than two centimetres by two centimetres. I remember staring at that tiny square for what seemed like a really long time. I am incredibly blessed to have so many amazing people in my life. I have people I can turn to for just about anything, in my business and personal life. I tried to add some of those names to the box, but kept removing them, knowing that though I valued their opinions in some ways, they didn't quite fit the title of being in my 'square squad'. When it came to who really mattered and the opinion of that person, the only name that I could truly write in the box, other than my own, was that of my husband.

Reflecting on this, looking at his name, the one and only name in my 'square squad' box I'm not surprised. Having now been married to my husband for over ten years I have never felt more at home in the presence of another human being. There is an unassuming energy that he creates that has given me a true sense of safety since the moment we started our relationship. He has withstood the arduous circumstances of being in a relationship with me as I continued to struggle with trauma, always providing me with a space to be unapologetically myself.

At times he has had to face my anger as I've ranted and raved about the injustice of the world, specifically yelling about men, white men and middle-aged white men, while he looked back at me identifying as said middle-aged white man. He has found a new way of communicating with me during these moments where, though he understands that the anger isn't directed at him, he has sometimes been wounded by the anger.

I'm sure he has disliked the bouts of anger, but the most heartbreaking part of our marriage is that he has lived through the trauma with me. Especially heartbreaking has been the way it has impacted me in the way of triggers, often caused by physical touch. My body carries the trauma and the reactions to triggers are involuntary. The trauma hijacks my body, holding it hostage. The distress for both of us when he has simply gone to touch my face or stand close to me and my body has winced or recoiled. The pain that we both experience at that moment, for me the trigger itself being sent into a state of shock where I have to disconnect the fight, flight or freeze mechanism, then the pain at realising I've reacted in this way and likely hurt him. But the worst pain of all is the rejection I see in his eyes, the hurt and confusion when he is time and time again pushed away by the woman he loves.

Watching him reach for me for over ten years whilst I recoil into myself has been a kind of torture that is hard to describe. I want to reach for him, to take his hand, to step out of the darkness. But the trauma freezes me there. The trauma holds me with a gun to my temple, telling me not to move, not to make a sound, reminding me we are trapped in this space together. Forever trapped in my body. I often feel like I'm watching us from outside of my body, watching the tragic love story of two people who love each other more than life itself ending up like magnets, two magnets who are the same, charged by their love but watching them repel, no matter how hard they try to be close to each other.

This physical distance is not the only heartbreak my husband experiences. When I retreat, falling back into behaviours of walls, boxes and masks I have emotionally pushed him away. After a lifetime of trauma and being hurt by the people closest to me I have defaulted to crawling inside of myself when things are hard, shutting everyone out to go it alone. This does not fare well for a loving, emotionally-connected relationship when I continually tell him that I don't need him or anyone else to support me, that I don't trust anyone and can do everything on my own. Nevertheless, with his perseverance, here we are, overcoming the trauma and continuing to build our lives together.

My husband has helped me build my island. He in many ways is one of the first foundation blocks of the space we now call home, for it's the safety he has gifted me, the purest of love, and the freedom for me to grow and for me to be the best version of myself that has given me the confidence to live here on my island with him and our family. When we began our relationship, we spoke of being in our bubble. I now know that it was our way to shield ourselves as I continued to live on the mainland. Our bubble has grown, and now encapsulates our entire island. Like our love, it only gets better the more we look after it and value its worth. On my bad days, I trust him to watch the shoreline, to keep our island safe, and to only lower the drawbridge for the ones who are welcome in our space. There is now no desire to create another life. I plan to spend the remainder of my life, this chosen version of my one life, with him on the beautiful island we built together.

Dear Husband,

This life we have created together is one of wonder and I don't believe I've had a day in the many years I've spent sharing my life with you where I have not been grateful for the man that you are and the way that you love me.

We have spoken many times about how we wonder if other couples in the world love each other the way you and I share our love. We have curiously talked about the special bubble that we've had and how it was the space that we first shared as we created the early years of our relationship.

I know we have something really special, but I also know our life together has come with many challenging moments that have constantly tested us. Challenges not only dished out by the outside world but by the trauma that has lived in me for so many years, the trauma that has caused me to bring some of those explosives from the mainland into our home at times, with you and our relationship being the casualties.

I'm sorry, so sorry that in being the woman you love I am also the woman who often causes you pain, rejection and heartbreak. I know that you understand the hurt I cause is not intended, though I know that this understanding does not make the hurt any less painful.

Thank you for withstanding the pain, thank you for showing me what life is like in a place of safety and for being one of the first foundations of our island.

Our island is the new version of the bubble we created in those early years. We share it with our children, we share it with our loved ones and our friends. But know that through this journey and in my healing, I am creating a place for just you and I on our island, where we can connect and be the magnets that no longer repel; we can be connected in a way we've always wished we were.

Thank you for being the incredible man that you are and for walking beside me as I've become the woman I am today. I am the best version of myself when I am sharing my life with you, and if you continue to share it with me, I plan to share my one life with you forever.

I love you.

Your Caroline

X

Twenty Seven

LOOKING OUT TO
ROUGH SEAS

I first learnt of a tsunami in 2004. It was the day after Christmas and the world heard the news of gigantic waves of water that hit the shorelines of Sri Lanka, Indonesia and Thailand. I had heard of gigantic waves before, always picturing the waves in places like Hawaii where pro surfers claimed their championships. But I had never heard of a wave that was caused by an earthquake, roaring up through the ocean, propelling massive volumes of water to unsuspecting shores.

Witnesses of this tsunami would recount that they watched the water recede back into the ocean, gathering its fury before returning with a power that would engulf everything in its path. I remember learning about this particular tsunami as many Australian travellers had been impacted by the devastation of this natural disaster. With over 230,000 lives lost in a matter of hours, the impact of this tsunami is currently recorded to be the deadliest in history.

When I think of the analogy of my island and the safe place I've created that I now call home, I am mindful that I am surrounded by water. In building this space for myself I am not always immune to the impacts of things that happen on the mainland. As my disclosures are revealed to more people, difficult conversations are had and triggers occur that cause explosions on the mainland, which can at times cause earthquakes. The seas between the mainland and my island can get rough in these moments and there have been times where the earthquakes have caused tsunamis, like the onslaught I experienced after my uncle revealed my story to family members and I was met with weeks of phone calls and messages. A tsunami of questions and opinions for me to withstand.

There are some days where the seas are rough but I can prepare myself to weather the storm ahead, however it is the unexpected tsunami that I fear the most. It's the one that could wipe me out as an individual, and it could also wipe out my island, which is in many ways still in its infancy, still being carefully built to withstand the years to come.

There are many challenges, some are triggers, prompted by the physical touch from loved ones which send me into a state of retreat and distress. There are recurring nightmares as I attempt a good night's sleep, causing me to wake in a sweat, my body face down, arms tightly by my side, blanket wrapped around me like a cocoon in defence against being touched in the night. There is the voice of the inner mean girl, who occasionally still whispers her poisonous words of: 'It's all your fault,' 'You did this,' 'Your body did this,' and 'Control your body and what it makes him do!' Then there is the shame that I am working to shift, though it occasionally returns and I feel an overwhelming sense of sadness that the abuse and trauma is the reality of my life.

The challenges that I'm often not prepared for are when the stormy seas send a bolt of lightning that strikes me with such force that I'm rendered numb for days at a time. These bolts of lightning have come from the people who often claim to love me the most. Their words and questions, which they believe are well intended, are like daggers, piercing me and filling me with a feeling of deep sorrow at the loss of trust in said person.

I have had extended family members ask me to stay quiet. I have had some who have expressed that they

A STORY OF SURVIVAL

would have likely made choices similar to my mother's. Some have uttered dismissive words such as, 'It's in the past, so why are we talking about this today?' and simply wanting me to 'Get over it.' One of these lightning strike moments came in a comment, which was not intended for my ears or spoken directly to me, where someone I genuinely loved and trusted said aloud, 'Why is she doing this? Is she planning to share her story so she can be famous?' I still gasp when I recall this statement, the shock of the strike still rendering me silent in those few moments as I grapple with the ice-cold insensitivity of comments like these.

No, I will not stay quiet.

No, I do not agree with my mother's choices and if I was put in a similar position as a mother, I would not have acted in the same way as her.

Yes, the abuse is in the past, but the trauma has lived with me for nearly 30 years, and may continue to forever. I carry it in my body. I cannot escape it and to make real change for the future I cannot ignore the ugliness anymore.

Yes, I can just get over it, but I also can't just get over it. That's the point; this isn't something static, it is a moving target, a lived experience that is a part of my lifelong journey.

No, fame is not in any way the desired outcome for me speaking my truth. I am very good at many things that

247

I've sought public recognition for. I've actively worked hard my entire life to *not* be known as the woman who was sexually abused by her father. So no, this is not about the perceived allure of fame. This is about something far greater than me. This is about change.

These are just a few examples of moments I have weathered and though in these moments I feel failed by some of the people that I love, I know I must survive these moments in order to continue enjoying the freedom of my island.

In addition to the storms I have weathered caused by loved ones, there is also the greater society that we live in and the pain that comes from the barrage of news stories just like mine. With the publicised work of the 'Me Too' Movement, the 'Time's Up' campaign and the more recent backlash in Australia where women have called on our government officials to make our society a safer place, there isn't a day that goes by without hearing of another sexual violence survivor.

Whilst listening to formidable voices like the one of Grace Tame, who has used her story of surviving childhood sexual abuse to make significant legislative changes and brought the topic of childhood sexual abuse to the forefront of the Australian public eye, it can be hard as a survivor to cheer for her success, fervently commending her courage whilst not being triggered and impacted personally.

It's a tough tightrope to walk. I look at the women in the world speaking up while they say, 'Enough is enough,' and commend them as I know how difficult it is to find the courage to press on. But at the same time, it can be overwhelming as I watch these women disclose, realising that in their truth lies an abuse of power and a level of corruption that is rife in our governments, schools, churches, sporting clubs, families and, yes, even in our very own homes. Similar to the individuals who occupy these organisations and collective bodies, these systems and institutions can be more than one thing; brilliant in their purpose and success and catastrophically flawed in their lack of accountability and justice for survivors.

It can be hard to keep listening to the voices that are sharing the truth, because the truth is ugly. To acknowledge it often means acknowledging our own moments of complicity and likely acknowledging that there is a person in our lives that has in the past or is currently abusing their power at the cost of a victim-survivor. If we continue to listen to the voices of survivors, we have to recognise that the perpetrators live among us, and that is deeply unsettling.

When it all becomes too much, I remind myself that I have had the power to survive up until this very day and that I have the power to continue to survive, even on the hardest of days. Even when the countless stories of survivors break my heart when I see and hear my story within theirs, I must continue to survive.

The only actions I can control are my own. I choose to open my door to fellow survivors so their truths can be heard. It is no mean feat to face this wave of truth. I watch as I add my truth to that sea of voices and do my best to brace myself if the tide one day recedes, and if one day the voices of truth become a deafening tsunami.

Despite the explosions, strikes of lightning and storms I have weathered, I have the capability to withstand whatever is to come. I will protect my island and the people who live here with me, and from my island, I will continue to be a voice for survivors who have not yet found their voice. I will stand on the shore; I will face the tsunami. I will survive another day.

Twenty Eight

WALK BESIDE ME

There are people in my life who have been supporting me during this more recent part of my healing journey. One of the questions they have asked, a question many people have asked me over the years, is how do they best support me on this difficult journey?

I can only share what has worked for me personally; not everyone will want or need the same type of support as I do, but as this is my story of survival, I can only share what I have lived. There will be supporters and survivors alike who do not agree with my path and I completely respect that, though I am not sharing my story to change their paths, I am simply living and travelling through my own journey one step at a time. As I've travelled on the path of healing there have been things that haven't worked, that have annoyed and angered me. There have been moments that have set me back or decisions that have taken me on the wrong path, but that has been a part of the human experience for me. I am reminded that these detours and roadblocks are the parts that make us all similar in our experience of life, although we are unique in our choices and chosen paths.

Language has power. I am always mindful of the words I choose when talking about my lived experience. In a similar way, I speak of 'the' trauma instead of 'my' trauma. The trauma is not mine, the survival is, so that is what I claim and how I choose to see myself as I continue on this journey. My biggest request as a survivor is that my supporters walk *beside me*. These words are specifically chosen. I believe there is a clear difference between walking ahead of someone, walking beside someone and walking behind someone. It is not as simple as walking with them. It is a choice in where you position yourself as their supporter.

As a mother, I have walked beside my children many times. During senior high school, my eldest son experienced a very difficult time and though I wanted to swoop in and be his saviour, I knew I couldn't. I had to walk beside him. Over the weeks of this crisis situation, he heard me say time and time again that I was walking beside him. One day in a moment of confusion and slight frustration he said 'Mum, why do you keep saying that with so much emphasis on the *beside* part, what do you mean?!'

I explained to him that I could not fix the problem he was facing if I attempted to forge ahead, fighting the battle for him and dragging him along the way he would not learn anything from the experience, and the problem may not actually be fixed at all. We would both walk that path exhausted, me tiring from dragging him and him feeling every bump and graze whilst being dragged on the path.

If I walked behind him, I may be tempted to catch him every time he stumbled, which would mean he would also not learn any of the lessons himself. In doing so, the experience would be pointless and the journey would likely take longer. Worse still, if I walked behind him, I could become a burden, expecting him to carry me as he journeyed on and I experienced emotions of disappointment that he was on this path in the first place. Him having to carry the burden of his disappointed mother and me being carried by my son was not a burden I was willing to put on him.

So instead, I was choosing to walk beside him. I would be his counsel when he needed to share his thoughts and ideas. I would endure the rocky path ahead, never judging the paths he chose but always there to encourage him along the way. I would never leave his side, even in the moments that were the hardest, but I would also not do the work *for* him.

There have been people in my life over the years who have attempted to be my saviours. Although in my childhood, in those very early years of the abuse, I well and truly needed to be saved and taken out of harm's way, this is no longer the case for me now as an adult. In the more recent years, as I have disclosed to different people, I have seen a few of them jump up in alarm. They react to my disclosure as if the abuse is happening to me right in front of their eyes and they are shocked into a state of high alert. This in itself is a trigger as I watch them experience their own version of fight, flight or freeze. In this case, their bodies choose to fight. Even when realising the abuse has ceased, they still seem to want to grab their torches and pitchforks, to gather an angry crowd and to march up the hill to slay the dragon. These are the people who want to walk 'ahead' of me; they want to fight the fight for me, instructing me on what to do next or attempting to shelter me from a dragon who stopped breathing fire many years ago. They do not see the scars from the years of withstanding the trauma. These are the people who have very vocal opinions on what I should do, and they sometimes choose to criticise me, pity me or simply be angry that I am 'Doing it all wrong.' They somehow convince themselves that they need to act now, to take control. That they need to save me, *today*. When they march ahead, determined to fix the issue at hand, they often look back at me, as they drag me along this path I did not choose to walk and pity me, wondering why I can't keep up their punitive, revenge-fuelled pace. This is not my path, and this is why I do not ask people to walk ahead of me.

Some people have claimed they want to walk with me, but are really walking on a very different path. They genuinely believe that they want to help, but they are scared of the truth and of the work that is involved in supporting someone who is experiencing healing after the trauma. These people have pretended to walk with me whilst looking over at me, occasionally throwing comments over to me on my path, comments that are intended to be words of encouragement. Like a lazy coach eating doughnuts on a buggy, riding on a path nearby shouting unhelpful comments through a megaphone. Though they make a point to never get too close, they continue to walk on their own path and to be honest their lack of real commitment to walking with me on my journey is why their opinions are none of my business.

There are people who have genuinely wanted to walk with me. They have meant well but had no idea what to do. These people find themselves confused and have a million questions, assuming that I have all of the answers. In addition to the questions, they attempt to encourage me with statements like 'You're so brave,' but this just makes the situation awkward as I did not plan any of this and I do not get up every day trying to be brave. Though these people want to walk with me, they end up being baggage. I have to drag them along as they question every next step I take, attempting to take steps directly after me, walking in the imprints of my footsteps on the path. At times I have to carry them as they cry over how sad they are for me. I do not have the capacity to carry them, or their displaced emotions.

After years of discovering that many people default to these positions, I have actively chosen to ask them to walk *beside me*. In walking *beside me*; they can accompany me along my journey, though they cannot map out the path ahead. I do not expect them to take charge nor do I expect them to know what route to take. This is my journey and at times even I do not know where we are headed. When they walk *beside me* at my pace we take the journey together, and if we come across a challenge, though I am the only person that can overcome the challenge at hand I know I have my supporters there to talk to, to share in my pain and to encourage me to keep going even when it is hard. When they walk *beside me*, they can also share in my joy. Similar to overcoming the challenges, they cannot create the joy but they can share it with me in a way a true comrade does.

When I explained this analogy to my son, I watched as he processed my words. As often happens with teenagers I sat wondering if I had spoken for too long, if my words had felt like a lecture to him. Then he looked back at me and said, 'Ah, I think I get it. You can't walk ahead of me because I won't learn anything and it will be annoying because I don't want you to lead me. You can't walk behind me, catching me every time I stumble as I also won't learn a thing. But you are walking beside me, and every time I stumble though it hurts you to watch me fall, you will wait with me, wait as I tie my shoes, dust myself off and get ready to walk again. Then you will walk beside me again. No matter how many times I stumble or take the wrong path you'll be there. It's the way you love me unconditionally.'

'Yes, that's it,' I said, tears welling in my eyes. 'It's the way I love you unconditionally.'

My journey of healing and the analogies I use in explaining that journey may not be for everyone. Some survivors may want to be carried, some may need to be caught. Personally, I need you to walk *beside me*. As you walk beside me on this journey of healing and accountability your role is to listen, your role is to believe my truth and your role is to be there, unconditionally.

Twenty Nine

DEAR SURVIVORS

There is a question that comes to mind when I hear the word 'survivor'. I think to myself, 'Aren't we all survivors?' There is an innate survival mechanism in all of us, it exists at the core of our human experience and it shows itself when we let out our first cry as a newborn. This cry for survival gives voice to this instinct that a newborn has for nourishment, protection and love. This is in all of us, and as we grow this survival mechanism grows with us.

Some of us survive against extreme odds, some live through war, some experience life-threatening physical violence, some are tortured mentally and go on to endure mental health issues. Some, like myself, live through life-and-death surgery to overcome significant medical issues. Then there are the lucky few who simply wake each day with little to no need to utilise their survival mechanisms.

I have had conversations with friends who genuinely do not believe they have ever had to survive. When I share my lived experience with them they express how grateful they are to have lived a relatively pain-free life. They live in their privilege; they were born into safe, happy families, where their physical and emotional needs were always met. They went on to attend school, and though they experienced some emotional and mental stretching during their adolescence, overall they passed through their childhood and young adult life relatively unscathed. Heading into their adult years they continued what I believe is a strange streak of luck, forging down their desired paths of creating a career and a family with minimal distress.

These people confuse me no end. At times I am angered by their lack of understanding, I'm frustrated at how lucky they are and how unlucky I am in comparison. What makes them so special that they have the privilege of not identifying as a survivor? Or more to the point, what makes me so unlucky, so damaged that I was destined for this life of trauma and ongoing self-directed healing and development?

Maybe these rare people live life the way that it is supposed to be. Maybe they are the example of what we could have if we found a way to reduce the trauma in the world. This would be a huge task when survival is something we humans continue to do, due to the many different types of trauma that exist.

I know in the past people have thought I was one of the lucky ones. Under the armour, speaking the lines from my well-rehearsed script, at times I had even convinced myself that I was one of them. Today I know the genuine lucky ones are few and far between. Though I envy their luck, if that's what we are calling it, my focus when it comes to the humans I connect with the most has always been the ones with lived experiences similar to my own. There is a sense of belonging and safety in our lack of luck.

It does not surprise me when I speak with someone and open up about my truth to have them share something similar in their own story. We've seen the statistics; we know that survivors walk among us every day. But these statistics have names, they are our sisters, they are our brothers, they are the people who we sit next to on the train. They are the human beings who have had to survive, so they can find a way to live their lives, to find a way to press on because the alternative is far too tragic.

In the statistics we read, we know that victim-survivors suffer significant ongoing trauma after the sexual abuse they experience. In *The Body Keeps the Score* Bessel van der Kolk speaks of how 'Traumatised people chronically feel unsafe inside their bodies: The past is alive in the form of gnawing interior discomfort. Their bodies are constantly bombarded by visceral warning signs, and, in an attempt to control these processes, they often become experts at ignoring their gut feelings and in numbing awareness of what is played out inside. They learn to hide from their selves.' This experience of the body reacting in this way can cause long-term PTSD resulting in poor mental health, eating disorders, self-harm and the most tragic of all results, suicide.

I have fought against my body keeping the score of my trauma. In doing so I have had to put many things in place over the years to assist me in my journey of healing. Though I do not claim to be an expert in the space of healing, I do know what has been helpful for me in the past.

Language matters, especially the language I have spoken to myself over the years. Shifting my mindset and my words from 'victim' to 'survivor' was incredibly important as to where I positioned myself in the trauma. The trauma isn't mine to keep, nor is the abuse. Being a victim is also not how I choose to see myself. I am stronger than the abuse, the trauma and the label of victim. I have chosen to be a survivor. It is no small feat I have survived childhood sexual abuse and gone on to thrive in my life. In choosing to survive, in choosing to show up every day and be the best version of myself that I can, I have been able to embrace the title of survivor and stand in the strength the title holds.

Even though selecting the language that serves me is one step of the process, unlearning is another. In dismantling the 'good girl' I have let go of the word 'should'. There is nothing that I 'should' do. There is choice, there are my values that guide these choices, but there are no longer pre-existing relationships or models that burden me to do things simply because I think I should. I am not obligated to do things the way they have always been done. It is clear to me that something needs to change, safety needs to be my priority and I need to protect my island so I can continue to thrive in that space of safety and freedom.

In doing so I have put boundaries in place to support my healing. Yes, I will admit at times the boundaries have been restrictive and have been the walls, boxes and masks I've spoken of. Regardless of when the boundaries were in place or what form they took on, they were designed to protect me. Even with the newest boundary of the drawbridge that allows visitors to my island, I am acutely aware that I have to enforce and protect my boundaries for them to exist and for them to be successful. It is often the moments where a well-meaning visitor comes to the edge of the drawbridge that I have to tune into the purpose of my boundaries and have to do my best to keep them in place if what the visitor is carrying will hurt me or my island.

To support myself and to live safely on my island I have a wonderful inner circle of family and friends. My husband is my closest ally and is the one I turn to first for his words of wisdom or simply as a sounding board. He cannot do the work for me, at times he cannot even hold the boundaries in place, but he can be there, walking beside me as I work hard to protect myself and the things that are important to me.

I always remember that it is ok to not be ok. In dismantling my armour in recent years, I often sit in the depths of my sorrow and pain, in the vulnerability of knowing that this particular day is one day where I do not feel ok. This is a journey; no two days are ever the same. I have learnt that to feel connected to my inner circle of people in my life I need to be vulnerable enough to let them in. For me, I've created my island. I've been incredibly selective as to who lives there or visits, that the members of my community align with my values and understand the importance of safety in my space.

To connect, to really feel connected, I choose to make space for them, I choose to open myself up. I choose not to be alone on the journey.

I have experienced various health issues during my life, though it is yet to be determined if they are all symptoms of the abuse. Trauma research has shown that there is likely a link between the trauma and the autoimmune disease that I have been diagnosed with, chronic fatigue. Over the years I have been mindful to listen to my body. Though my body has been my enemy at times, carrying the trauma, keeping the score, it has also carried me on my journey all these years. When I listen to it, I know when to rest. I know when to cry and I know when I need to laugh and be with people who provide me with the space to do both, to be both joyous and sad, whatever my body needs.

Finding my voice and sharing my truth has been the biggest fight in my story of survival. The voice I found as a teenager when I disclosed the abuse to my mother. The voice I found when I shared my truth with friends throughout my lifetime. The voice that shook as I shared my truth with my husband, after pushing him away one too many times. This voice that sometimes trembles, even today, is mine and it has the power to change my world. Every time I share my truth and my lived experience of trauma I do so in the hope that I will create a space for another survivor to do the same. Our stories matter. We do not need to shout to be heard, we need to speak, one clear word at a time. It takes practice, but every time my voice gets stronger, my story makes more of a difference.

I am terrified, but I know that I cannot be brave if I am not also terrified. More than one thing can be true even in my bravery. I choose to keep going on this journey even when it is hard because I know that I can make a difference. My story has already made a difference in the lives of survivors, and even if it hadn't, sharing my story has made a difference to my life. My story has made me a survivor.

Dear Survivors,

I see you. I believe you. I walk beside you.

Wherever you are in your journey I want you to know that you are not alone. There is a family of survivors here in the world who hold you in the safety of their love and support. We hold you and the version of you that you were on the first day the abuse began, the day that your life changed forever. We hold you as you grieve that version of yourself and we walk beside you as you find the strength to carry on.

Your story is unique. Only you can understand the tragedy that has occurred, but you have a fire in you that has brought you to this very day. You are a survivor and no matter how many obstacles the world continues to throw your way, you can continue further down your path of healing. Only you can survive the abuse, only you can heal from the trauma, that is your superpower.

There will be people in your life who mean well as they attempt to support you, though they may end up disappointing you. Please don't shut out the world because of the few who don't meet your needs. There are so many good people in the world, but they can't be there for you and they can't walk beside you if you don't let them in. Love can only grow from a place of love. I love you, and I know that you love yourself too. Take that love and open up space for more of it, open up space to let someone else love you. You are worthy of the highest level of life and love.

We are experiencing the ongoing journey of life and in choosing to show up every day there will be good days and bad. There will be days when it all feels too hard to carry on. All of these days are a part of the journey, but you, my friend are stronger than your darkest days. You do not need to look too far ahead down the path. Stand true in yourself, stand in these footsteps you have right here, today at this moment and remember that you are doing the best you can in your survival. Just do not give up, the world needs you.

As a survivor I need you. I need your collective love and strength so I can carry on. You are a part of my family.

I see you. I believe you. I walk beside you.

I love you. I am you.

Caroline

x

Thirty

I DO NOT HAVE THE ANSWERS

I do not have the answers. I wish I did; it would make life so much easier, not only for myself but for the millions of survivors out there in the world. There are a few types of change that I'm focusing on as I continue to walk the path of my own healing journey. My focus is on eliminating the silence of survivors and creating transparency and accountability as we identify perpetrators. I am also exploring and attempting to gain an understanding of the space between rehabilitation and retribution for these perpetrators. Most of all, I am focused on supporting survivors as we all continue to heal.

I'm curious to see a change in how we view survivors. I believe we need to see them as the courageous humans that they are. Though I know that first, it is an inside job. I've experienced that I personally needed to see a change in myself, to see myself as a survivor, before others can see me in that way. I am living proof that someone can step outside of being a victim and truly claim their place as a survivor. Language matters and it is important that we respect the language and position that each individual victim-survivor chooses. Over the recent years, I have begun to use my story and my voice for good, to find avenues to share my experience and to open doors for others to do the same. For me, I believe that in eliminating silence on the matter of childhood sexual abuse, we can begin to dismantle the systems that create the abuse in the first place.

Eliminating silence does not need to occur only in the ways I've chosen to share my story. The silence is eliminated once a survivor chooses to disclose. The first conversation is the most important one. It is the beginning, the moment in time that starts to give the survivor back their power as it begins to shift the shame of the abuse. In speaking openly about my experience, I hope to set an example for others to do the same.

In reading through the lived experiences of the contributors in the *Love with Accountability* anthology, I know my story is not entirely unique. Like me, there are many survivors who have been sexually abused by a parent. Yes, I have spoken to countless survivors. So far, only one has a story just like mine, a story of her father being more than one thing. But sadly, as the stories in *Love with Accountability* have shown me, there are countless stories out there like mine. They are buried under an additional layer of shame that comes with the word incest. Even writing that word makes my stomach churn a little, it paints such horror in the truth of my story and labels my experience with something our society deems to be so disgusting and inexcusable that it fills me with shame to know my life has that word in it. This shame is further compounded by the lack of understanding of this matter, or more to the point, the lack of understanding of how common this type of abuse is. Nevertheless, I choose to speak up. Because the silence creates more pain, the silence creates a place where perpetrators thrive and their actions become commonplace.

I genuinely believe the first step in our change is using our voices, though this not only applies to survivors, it applies to the bystanders as well. As adults we have a duty of care, we all have children in our lives for whom we have a responsibility. We may not be their parents, but as they are the future of humanity, as they are the future of ourselves, we owe it to them to be safe adults.

We owe it to them to speak up, even when it makes us and the people around us uncomfortable.

We need to empower children to have autonomy over their bodies. We can begin by teaching them that their bodies are theirs and theirs alone. That they have the right to choose how to use their bodies, and if their instincts tell them that they don't want to hug, kiss or even stand next to someone who makes them uncomfortable, we must empower them to have the right to choose. When their voices are small, small like their innocent child-sized bodies, we must speak for them, tuning into their intuitions to know when they are uncomfortable. We must ask them how they feel and we must speak for them to say no, they do not wish for their bodies to be made to comply, simply to be polite.

Language has power, and in teaching our children and equipping them with their words, they will have more of a chance to understand how to use their words when their safety is at risk. Do not ask your children to be silent, do not tell them that children should be seen and not be heard. You will create a voiceless child, and a voiceless child cannot say no. Explain to them how their bodies work, what areas are private, what touches are good or bad and speak of the risks involved in keeping secrets.

They are smarter than what we believe, they are much more capable than what we give them credit for.

By using real, straightforward language when discussing our bodies, their bodies will remove the opportunity for confusion in the future. We do not want to create shame around their bodies or their sexuality, because in creating that shame in their bodies, we create a space for silence, and this space is where perpetrators plant the first seeds of their grooming. Shame can become an infestation, where terrible things happen under the blanket of silence and secrets.

There are incredible organisations working to empower our children to recognise these insidious grooming behaviours. The work of Hetty Johnston and the team at Bravehearts not only supports survivors of abuse but also teaches educators, parents and adults to create safer spaces for our children.

In addition to the work with survivors and adults, they work with young people aged 12 to 18, who have shown signs of, or have engaged in harmful sexual behaviour. Research has shown that there are a wide variety of reasons why young people engage in harmful behaviour, so with their Turning Corners program, Bravehearts are looking to intervene in these early stages to reduce the risk of these young people becoming long-term perpetrators. They believe that in addressing the whole cycle of sexual abuse and assault, we can truly prevent child sexual abuse from occurring.

In addition to the work being done with young people who show signs of being potential harm-doers, we cannot ignore the people in our community who are already doing harm. The statistics show us that in a similar way that survivors walk among us, so do the perpetrators. If we continue to ignore them then this problem continues to exist.

I do not have the answers. Nor do I expect every victim-survivor to agree with my thoughts on these matters. First and foremost, the survivor, their healing and their safety need to be the highest priority for us to heal as a collective. For some, healing will come in the form of criminal justice and I respect the need for that.

I personally haven't pursued the path of criminal justice. I have a very detailed and educated understanding of how my experience of abuse would be managed within that system. I have spoken to the respective authorities and understand that the path of criminal justice is one that I have a full right to take. However, I don't believe that path will serve me in my healing. As I use the neuroplasticity of my brain and attempt to rewire the pathways of the triggers I experience and the ways in which the trauma impacts my life, I don't believe that going to court and sending my father to jail is the answer to my healing. Reliving the trauma within a criminal justice system, having to recount the specific physical aspects of the abuse and being questioned by strangers is not the path I choose to take.

If we look at the numbers, I also question how we create a criminal justice system to house the millions of perpetrators in the world. The sheer numbers and lack of resources in this model simply do not add up.

I personally seek restorative justice, knowing that I may never actually receive it. That is the path I feel may take me to a place of peace. I do not wish harm on my father, nor do I wish him to die in a jail cell. But I do wish for him to heal and for him to find a way to address the triggers that cause him to be a perpetrator. If there is a cure for that poison that causes him to do harm, I wish that he could receive it.

But similar to the change in how we view survivors, starting with how they view themselves, if perpetrators are to change - if they are to be rehabilitated - it starts with them. It takes a level of accountability and self-awareness that cannot be created by anyone other than themselves. Within a restorative justice system, both parties can heal, but only once the perpetrator is accountable for the harm they have caused and only when they actually *want* to change. In addition to these two parties, it is then the responsibility of the community to continue to hold accountability and transparency as their key values, not only for the safety of the original survivor but for the safety of the entire community.

In eliminating my silence, I have begun to create transparency and accountability. I am learning more about the space between rehabilitation and retribution and I have a greater understanding of restorative justice. I have not commenced a restorative justice process with my father; we just aren't there yet. As I continue to survive the pain of my truth, I know there is hope, and in that hope, there is healing.

Thirty One

DEAR SONS

As I actively work on being the best version of myself, I am mindful that I am more than one thing. Becoming a mother at the age of 21 has been pivotal to my journey as a survivor. Prior to the day I held my first-born son in my arms, I didn't truly know a love like it. There is an extraordinary unspoken bond between a mother and their child. I struggle to find the words to describe the feelings of protection, wonder and unconditional love that I feel for my sons.

Becoming a mother in my early twenties was my first experience of a breakdown. This breakdown happened gradually over a few years but started when my son was born and my then-husband and I needed financial support. As we lived on the mainland and still had deep connections with my birth family it seemed logical to lean on them for support and to move in with my parents when my son was born. Yes, that meant moving into the home where the abuse had occurred and it meant having my parents around us daily. Looking back, it was clear that this decision, in addition to the shift in me moving from being an individual to someone forever connected to another human being as a mother, was incredibly pivotal to the start of my breakdown.

Soon after we lived in that house with our son, I started to get sick. Not physically sick, but my mental health was deteriorating by the second. I had received information from the maternal health nurse about the baby blues and postnatal depression but what I was experiencing didn't seem to fit these descriptions. It was clear that something needed to change and in what seemed like an overnight decision we suddenly decided to find our own home and start our lives together in a new space. I thought that this would be enough, though I don't think I actually realised at the time that I was deep in a breakdown.

Even the change of location didn't seem to be enough; my parents continued to visit their first-born grandchild, and we continued to have a relationship with them. All the while my mental health continued to break down. Then one day, in what felt like shattering glass, I was hitting rock bottom, and something in me broke. I couldn't get out of bed for days and I remember my then-husband not knowing what to do. So, I sought a psychologist, the first one I had seen since seeing the psychologist I'd been sent to after disclosing to my mother when I was 16 years old. To think that in this eight-year period between when I was 16 to turning 24 that I had not sought any further professional support baffles me. I had also not disclosed the abuse to anyone other than my then-husband. The trauma had already caused intimacy issues in our relationship and had fractured us in a way that was significant in the future demise of our marriage. Looking back, I am sure that living on the mainland whilst continuing to live under the shame of the secret, it was glaringly obvious that things were terribly wrong. I had not only convinced myself but also everyone around me that I was ok, and that simply wasn't true.

It was clear that becoming a mother had changed me and that I had begun living in a whole new world. I was still attempting to balance my life on the mainland whilst navigating my new world as a mother. On the mainland I was a good girl, I was an obedient daughter, attempting to maintain normalcy for my parents, for myself and for my son. Attempting to retain the connection we had, the family I wanted so badly. Though the other world I lived in was one driven by instincts, this one was driven by an overwhelming, uncontrollable need to protect my son. The breakdown came in me trying to understand how my parents did not have the same instincts as me or, more specifically, how they chose not to act in the same way I believed I would, now that I was in their position; I was a parent.

Over the years I had walked the tightrope between these two worlds. Even years later, after identifying the need to be safe, marrying my now husband and actively working on being the best version of myself so I could be the best mother to my sons, I continued to walk the tightrope. I balanced between wanting my sons to have a relationship with their grandparents whilst also wanting to fiercely protect them, knowing that if what had happened to me happened to my sons, my actions would be vastly different to the actions of my parents.

It has taken being a mother for 15 years for me to put myself and the way I choose to show up as a mother before the way I show up as a daughter. When I chose to put myself first, as a mother, I automatically put my children first as I have gifted us a new life on our island.

Today I know that I am the best mother I can be to my sons. I am exactly who I need to be on this very day. Although there is a part of me that is terrified by the thought of them reading my words and hearing the pain of my story, this is exactly what I was meant to do. There is freedom for all of us outside of the silence.

My eldest son and I have spoken about the trauma. He is a young man now and our relationship continues to evolve in this space of truth and safety. As my younger son reaches the same age, I will prepare to share my truth with him also. I have nothing to hide here on our island.

As they get older, I know I am now leading by example by living a life that is true to my values, and in doing so that I am creating a space for them to also be free. Free of the obligations that come from the titles we are given when we become a mother or a son. They are free to live in truth and outside of silence. There is always an opportunity to speak about the truth, to have open conversations, to understand the complexities of more than one thing being true. I will always encourage them to ask questions, to seek real answers, and to form their own opinions on these complex matters, as they are individuals that are capable of so much more than what I give them credit for at times.

In creating our island, I have invited them to walk beside me. Though they may not know it, they are by far two of the most important people in my support team. They share that unspoken bond with me; they share my journey and they share our unconditional love.

Dear Sons,

You are the living, breathing example of what life can be like outside of silence. Though in your individual experiences you have known different versions of me I believe that there is a real understanding between us and that you know how much I love you both.

I know that with the boundaries I have placed around each of you and around our island, and with the values that I have instilled in the space we call home, you have grown to know the importance of being the best version of yourself and doing better when you know better.

Similar to how you walk beside me on my journey, I can only do the same for you. Though as your mother I wish I could protect you from the harm that life will likely bring, I cannot live your life for you, I can only walk beside you and I will do so with such pride, even when we reach challenging points in the road ahead.

There will be moments where you make mistakes. Accountability will be your key to repairing any damage that you have done. Remember to always do the right thing, even when it is hard. I hope you have seen that in me sharing my truth that it is me showing you how to actively do the right thing, even when it is hard.

You both are a significant part of my legacy, in being my sons, in showing up in our relationship the way that you show up, you are showing me that we can break cycles. We can repair the damage and pain of our ancestors and begin to heal the trauma. We are our ancestors' wildest dreams.

Thank you for opening my eyes to the beauty that is being your mother. When my days have been the hardest it is the two of you that have been the motivation I have needed to keep walking. Our unconditional love and the want I have for you both to be safe is why I keep walking through the journey of my healing.

In healing myself I hope to be the best version of myself, I hope to be the mother you have always wanted and the mother you will always need me to be.

I cannot express how much I love you both. There simply are no words. Know that I love you more each day and I will forever walk beside you.

I love you

Mum x

Thirty Two

WHY WE NEED YOUR SUPPORT

Psychologist and researcher Peter Levine is quoted to have said, 'You cannot do it alone, and nobody can do it for you.' This quote is a great way of describing the complexities of the survivor journey and the struggle in finding inner strength in self and also in needing a community around us. This insight is another way of emphasising the power of walking *beside* a survivor.

As I have taken you on this journey with me, you may now have a greater understanding of what it is like to live as a survivor, or more specifically, as a survivor of incest. You may now recognise someone in your life who identifies as a sexual abuse survivor. Or you may have recognised elements of your own story as you have read my words, walking beside me through these pages. You may now have the words to describe how you will walk beside the survivors in your own life on their journey of healing.

There are various roles that are needed in the support team of a survivor. For me personally, I have worked with various psychologists over the years to gain further insights into my emotions and mental state at the different stages of my life. Today I am working with a psychologist who specialises in trauma and uses person-centred cognitive behavioural therapy. I have also recently worked with another psychologist who has supported myself and my family members within the setting of family therapy. In addition to this support, I have a coach who assists me in my leadership, to enable me to lead myself as a survivor. She supports me as I show up in my community as a leader. There is also my physical health, with practitioners and support people in place to ensure my body is healthy so I can continue to practice my healing work. This team is accompanied by my husband, my children, and other family and friends who are all walking beside me as my support team.

You may be wondering what the path looks like for you as you walk beside the survivors in your life. In my experience, I believe there are specific things that you can do as a supporter of a survivor that can be of benefit to both of you and can further enrich the relationship you have.

The first step is believing survivors, in truly listening to us, especially when we first disclose the abuse and trauma to you. This moment in itself is incredibly important and though we understand it is difficult for you to hold this truth in your hands, it is vital that you hold it carefully as it comes with a sensitivity that can shatter if not handled with care. There is often lots of pre-planning in our minds before we disclose to you. Even in the moments when our disclosure is shared in a burst of anger or rage, there has likely still been many hypothetical conversations we have played out in our minds before the words leave our mouths.

We also need you to believe us. We can then build on the trust that moment will bring to further trust you and share more with you in our moments of vulnerability as we continue to heal. As you may have recognised in my story, there have been different points in my journey where I have needed specific support. As a child and young teen, during the time of the abuse, I needed safe adults to be aware of the abuse and to act with a duty of care. I needed them to intervene to stop the abuse from continuing. As a teenager, post the abuse, I needed safe adults to remove me from the traumatic environment and to encourage me to seek trauma-specific therapy to reduce the ongoing triggers and health implications. Today as an adult, I need your empathy, kindness and patience as you walk beside me in my support team.

When adult victim-survivors in your life choose to disclose and it is at a time where the abuse is still occurring, please give them the space to talk through their options to find safety. Be patient with them and please remember you cannot do the work for them. Do not forge ahead on a path and drag them along. You may not be able to be their saviour and in turn, may do more damage if you march ahead making decisions on their behalf. Their safety is the number one priority, but that safety is not only their physical safety, but their emotional and mental safety also. Support them to seek safety, be patient with them and most of all remember that you are walking beside them.

Encourage their self-care, support them in finding ways to look after themselves, and if possible, help them find space to actively perform their radical self-care. That may mean assisting them with child care, cooking meals for them, or simply being someone to cry with when the days are hard. Each individual survivor will need something different in the form of their self-care. When the individual's load is heavy and other matters of life need to be attended to, self-care can take a back seat, and they may need your support to make self-care a priority.

The support for children is different. If you believe there is a child being abused at this point in time and that they are in immediate danger or risk I encourage you to call the police. I must stress the importance of this matter, though you may not believe it is your place to do so or you may have other ideas instead of pursuing the criminal justice route, the police are the best people equipped with managing this matter if it is currently occurring. There are also clear mandatory reporting requirements for specific occupations, which are different in each state and territory of Australia. If you require clarification about who has to report, you can find detailed information via the Australian Institute of Family Studies. If you are unsure of this route or if you have a child that discloses to you and they are not in immediate danger, Bravehearts has comprehensive information on how to best respond to a child if they disclose to you and how to manage the next steps.

When supporting victim-survivors, remember you cannot be everything to us. You can be more than one thing, but not everything. Identify who and what you are in our support team and do that role to the best of your ability. If you stretch yourself too thin or try to take on a support role that you cannot actually fulfil, this is detrimental to both of us. Be honest with us. When you are finding things difficult, you can share this with us. All I ask is that you remember that it is not our job to carry you. You are walking *beside* us.

Respect our boundaries. Though you are a part of the support team, each member of that team has a different role to play and we may have different boundaries in place for each of those roles. As I've shared, my husband is the first point of call for me and he experiences walking beside me very differently to how my friends do. There is a level of intimacy, vulnerability and trust that we have that I simply do not have the capacity to have with multiple people. Yes, I trust my friends but there are roles they play in my support team that are sometimes purely to bring me joy, to share in the light-hearted moments of life and to laugh with me. You too can be the supporter that shares in joy. You don't need to take it all on or only focus on the dark days.

Lastly, respect our decisions. You may not agree with them, but this is our lived experience, our journey of healing. This is our story and we thank you for being a part of it. We do not want to do it alone. We want to belong to you and our greater community but to do this together we must do this for ourselves in our own way, with our own steps forward whilst you walk beside us.

Thirty Three

MORE THAN ONE THING CAN BE TRUE

There is a complexity to me and my life that I didn't really understand prior to writing these words. In sharing my experience, I have in many ways taken significant steps ahead in my healing journey. By choosing to share my truth I have and will continue to have many reasons behind the 'why' of why I share. I know that my words and my story can make a change. I know this because I have experienced this very change in the days of writing these words. In reading the words of survivors, I have learned so much about myself and I have found courage and strength that only comes from a space of truth.

Though I am nearing the end of my thirties, and though the abuse itself began when I was 10, I know that I still have a long way to go and so much more to learn. I will make mistakes; I will be a survivor but I may also upset and hurt people along the way. I can be more than one thing. In raising my hand up and speaking my truth I can only do this in my own way. I am leading by example, in the way that I wished someone close to me had led me when I was younger.

I am showing up for the younger versions of myself, giving them a voice and showing them that the woman they have become is ready and willing to make real change.

I am modelling that change, not only to myself but to my children who are by far the most important people in my life. I cannot expect of others what I am not willing to do to myself, so here I am using my voice in hopes that my story could mean that one adult will make a change that creates safety for one child. This can be the beginning of real change. I use my voice in hopes a fellow survivor will step out of their silence. I share my experience so supporters can do better, because they may now know better.

Every day will be different, I have known this all my life and I have been reminded further of this as I have shared my truth with you. Some of you may have shed a tear with me whilst reading my story. I have shed those same tears as I have sat and recounted the tragic moments of my life. There have been days that I have dug deep in the well of my fear to find the bravery I have needed to keep showing up to share with you. This well is not dry; there is more work ahead and I know I need to continue to embrace my fear so I can continue to be brave. I will continue to show up and share my story in the moments that matter.

My story and the work I have done around it is exactly what I have needed to do. I am doing the best I can with the tools and lessons that life has given me. Every day I will continue to heal in the space I have created outside of the silence and in my truth.

I am navigating a whole new world. It is terrifying not having a mask to protect me. I know that the masks are just another tool for silence, they carry shame and I will no longer be guilted into carrying that shame. In the truth and transparency of my words, I will find sanctuary on my island, even when the seas are rough and the world outside is an ugly place where the abuse of power and corruption live on.

As I add my voice to the sea of survivor stories, I ask you to be an ally to us. There is a chorus of voices just like mine who are still hurting and need your ears to listen. Most of all, there is a world full of innocent children who deserve to be free of the pain we have experienced. They do not need to live a life of abuse and trauma like ours. They deserve the freedom and innocence of their childhood.

I have been and will continue to be more than one thing. We can choose to be the good things. We can choose to show up in the world and do better.

In my legacy, with the impact I make in the world I need to be known for more than the abuse. I encourage you to see my story as one of hope. I am no longer silent today because I have found strength, I have found my survivor family and I now have my supporters walking beside me.

Today I sit in the peace of my integrity. I look back on the photos of that young girl and I know exactly who she is. She is more than one thing. She is the girl that will one day become the woman who finds her voice.

She is the girl that is a survivor. She is me.

ACKNOWLEDGEMENTS

To you, the reader. Thank you for being here with me as we've taken this journey together, right to the end of my memoir. Thank you for holding my words in your hands and in your heart. Thank you for walking beside me.

To my hilarious ride or die writing coach Holly, who would have known that we would have so much fun whilst writing this heartbreaking yet inspiring memoir? Thank you for walking beside me through the various drafts of words, holding my hand and nudging me along when I wanted to call it quits. Our endless voice memos and messages to each other will forever be saved in my phone for me to look back on this time and know what it is truly like to be supported with empathy, love and lots of laughter.

To my publishing team, to Kerry my designer, you really saw the beauty and hope in my story. Your cover design takes my breath away every time I see my book and I'll forever be grateful for you capturing the messaging in such a beautiful design.

To Karen, my editor, thank you for your kindness and support. You have taken my words and lifted them to a whole new level. I felt so held by you throughout the editing process and thank you for walking beside me through these final stages.

To Michael, not only have you supported me through the last steps to turn this manuscript into an actual, real-life book, but you were also the person who shared some truly insightful words with me back in 2019. Those words were the tipping point to so many significant changes in my life. Thank you, you may never really know how much of a difference you have made to my story.

To my Organise.Curate.Design. team, there have been a few of you over the past few years, but each and every one of you have provided me with so much love and support. Thank you for carrying on and being the marvellous humans that you are, especially when I was out of action working on my manuscript.

A special mention to Tahlia; you've been such a wonderful support over the past few months of this journey and there have been days where I really don't think I could have done it without you.

To the various people who read my manuscript in its different forms over the past year, thank you. Your time and care with my story will forever be something I am grateful for. The feedback you provided me, especially the feedback from my beta readers Caroline, Nicola and Sharon, helped me turn my draft into a manuscript that was worthy for a greater audience. To Julie, Ang and Hala, who also provided reviews and their thoughts, thank you for your words of support and for seeing the hope in my story.

To Kemi, our journey together has been mind-blowing. Thank you for being an incredible coach and someone who I now have the pleasure of calling a friend. I love you, you have walked beside me as I have become the woman I am today and I know that my transformation over the years has been due to your guidance and support.

To all of the family and friends who have cheered me along and sat with me as we have had deep thoughtful discussions on the various topics raised in my memoir, thank you. There are too many of you to name but I hope you know how much I appreciate you.

Thank you to my uncle who shared his story with me and trusted me in sharing it within my memoir.

A special shout out to Sally and Ray, Lisa, Harry, Jon, The Legends, My Project Gen Z Family and the women of Stealing Horses. You have walked beside me on some really dark days and I love you all so much.

To my siblings, sometimes I simply do not have the words to express how much I love you both. The words are not big enough, they do not come close to how much I appreciate your support and how grateful I am that you are both walking beside me. Thank you for everything, I love you.

To our dogs, the late Sam who was always my go-to for comfort over the years, thank you for all of the love you gave me in the time we had together. To Spike, my gentle giant, thank you for watching over me on those long days of writing and for the secret cuddles when Louie wasn't looking. To my Louie, thank you for simply being you, I didn't think I could love a dog the way I love you but the comfort and love you have brought me in the short time you've been by my side is phenomenal. You have sat with me on some of my hardest days of grief, thank you for being such a beautiful soul my little one.

To my incredible husband Blake, I could not have asked for a better partner in life. You have walked beside me throughout some of the most challenging days of my life and have continued to be my north star when the fog was so thick that I couldn't see the steps ahead of me. My north star to our island, my north star home to you, where I am free to be the best version of myself. I love you.

Lastly, to my boys, thank you for simply being the wonderful young men that you are. Your patience and love throughout the past few years has been incredible and I'm so proud of you both as I watch you become the men you are going to be. In a similar way to this book being dedicated to my ten-year-old self, this book is for you. The past two years have been the most challenging years of my life, but in sharing my truth I hope to make this world a safer place for you, and your children one day. Thank you for walking beside me, please know I will forever walk beside you too. My love for you is endless and unconditional.

ENDNOTES

Chapter 2 – CAROLINE, THE CHILD

- https://bravehearts.org.au/what-we-do/research/
  child-sexual-abuse-facts-stats/prevalence-of-child-
  sexual-abuse/
- Book by Bessel Van Der Kolk, The Body Keeps the
  Score https://www.besselvanderkolk.com/resources/
  the-body-keeps-the-score
  Also referenced in chapter 29.

Chapter 6 – HOW DID I STAY

- https://www.greekboston.com/culture/mythology/
  pandoras-box/

Chapter 9 – HUMAN SACRIFICE

- https://www.sciencemag.org/news/2018/06/feeding-
  gods-hundreds-skulls-reveal-massive-scale-human-
  sacrifice-aztec-capital

Chapter 11 – DISCOVERY IN CAMBODIA

- https://www.history.com/topics/cold-war/the-khmer-rouge

Chapter 12 – THE DEPTHS OF ANGER

- https://bravehearts.org.au/what-we-do/research/child-sexual-abuse-facts-stats/prevalence-of-child-sexual-abuse/

Chapter 15 – DEAR LITTLE SISTER

- https://en.wikipedia.org/wiki/The_Truman_Show#Plot

Chapter 17 – MY ISLAND

- Book by Glennon Doyle, Untamed https://untamedbook.com/

Chapter 21 – ANCESTRAL TRAUMA AND THE NEW GENERATION

- https://en.wikipedia.org/wiki/Mauritius
- https://www.roughguides.com/mauritius/west-coast/
- https://www.bbc.com/future/article/20190326-what-is-epigenetics

Chapter 22 – LIFE OUTSIDE OF SILENCE

- https://www.poetryfoundation.org/poetrymagazine/poems/154671/perhaps-we-are-our-ancestors-wildest-dreams?utm_source=twitter&utm_medium=social_media&utm_campaign=general_marketing

Chapter 24 – MY FATHER, IT'S TIME TO SAY GOODBYE

- https://www.aihw.gov.au/getmedia/0375553f-0395-46cc-9574-d54c74fa601a/aihw-fdv-5.pdf.aspx?inline=true
- https://aifs.gov.au/publications/adult-victimsurvivors-childhood-sexual-assault
- https://www.rainn.org/news/grooming-know-warning-signs

Chapter 27 – LOOKING OUT TO ROUGH SEAS

- https://www.history.com/news/deadliest-tsunami-2004-indian-ocean

Chapter 30 – I DO NOT HAVE THE ANSWERS

- https://www.lovewithaccountability.com/about-lovewithaccountability
- https://bravehearts.org.au/
- https://bravehearts.org.au/turningcorners
- https://www.iirp.edu/defining-restorative/restorative-justice-typology

Chapter 31 – DEAR SONS

- https://www.poetryfoundation.org/poetrymagazine/poems/154671/perhaps-we-are-our-ancestors-wildest-dreams?utm_source=twitter&utm_medium=social_media&utm_campaign=general_marketing

Chapter 32 – WHY WE NEED YOUR SUPPORT

- https://aifs.gov.au/cfca/publications/mandatory-reporting-child-abuse-and-neglect
- https://bravehearts.org.au/responding-to-disclosures-of-child-abuse/?fbclid=IwAR2iTotNSRwKdUkxOPyY3bZSciARPKJiBpu4ZG8s45f26ZbFo-DDrIhU9NY

RESOURCES

- NASASV (National Association of Services Against Sexual Violence) – https://www.nasasv.org.au/
- 1800 RESPECT (National Sexual Assault & Domestic Family Violence Counselling Service) – https://www.1800respect.org.au/
- Bravehearts (Protecting Australian Children against sexual abuse) – https://bravehearts.org.au/
- Blue Knot (Empowering recovery from complex trauma) – https://blueknot.org.au/
- SAMSN (Supporting Male Survivors of Childhood Sexual Abuse) – https://www.samsn.org.au/
- BRISSC – Brisbane Rape & Incest Survivor Support Centre – https://brissc.org.au/
- Act for Kids – https://www.actforkids.com.au/
- Daniel Morcombe Foundation – https://danielmorcombe.com.au/

- The Carly Ryan Foundation – https://www.carlyryanfoundation.com/
- Kids Helpline – https://kidshelpline.com.au/

www.ingramcontent.com/pod-product-compliance
Lightning Source LLC
Chambersburg PA
CBHW031927090426
42811CB00040B/2399/J